YOUTH
FUNDRAISERS

YOUTH FUNDRAISERS

RAISING MONEY THAT COUNTS

Lynn Strother Hinkle

Abingdon Press
Nashville

YOUTH FUNDRAISERS:
Raising Money That Counts

Copyright © 1995 by Abingdon Press

ISBN 0-687-01010-1

Library of Congress Cataloging-in-Publication Data

Hinkle, Lynn Strother.
    Youth fundraisers : raising money that counts / Lynn Strother.
      p.   cm.
    Includes index.
    Summary: Presents over 100 money-making ideas and projects for use with church youth groups and organizations.
    ISBN 0-687-01010-1 (pbk : alk. paper)
    1. Church group work with teenagers. 2. Church fund raising.
    [1. Church fund raising. 2. Moneymaking projects.] I. Title.
    BV4447.H55   1995
    254.8—dc20   95-18579
                                                           CIP
                                                           AC

The following fundraisers are adapted from *Directions in Faith* and are used by permission:

"Holiday Dinner"—MAM 1993— © 1992 Cokesbury; "Coffee Treats"—Spring 1990— © 1989 Graded Press; "Bake Sale"—Fall 1989— © 1988 Graded Press; "Other-Handed Cookie Sale"—Fall 1990— © 1990 Graded Press; "Super Bowl Subs"—Winter 1990-1991— © 1990 Graded Press; "Great Cake-Tasting Party"—Fall 1986— © 1986 Graded Press; "Chocolate Dreams"—Summer 1987— © 1987 Graded Press; "Strawberry Patch"—Spring 1987— © 1987 Graded Press; "Southern Nights"—Spring 1987— © 1986 Graded Press; "Family Fun Night"—Winter 1990-1991— © 1990 Graded Press; "Lip Sync Contest"—Spring 1991— © 1990 Graded Press; "Host a Hoe-Down"—JJA 1994— © 1994 Cokesbury; "Celebrity Look-Alike"—Summer 1988— © 1988 Graded Press; "Treasure Hunt"—Summer 1988— © 1988 Graded Press; "Sports, Anyone?"—Winter 1986-1987 ("Tennis Anyone?")— © 1986 Graded Press; Winter 1988-1989 ("Benefit Ball Game")— © 1988 Graded Press; "Valentine Messages"—Winter 1987-1988— © 1987 Graded Press; "A Valentine's Banquet"—Winter 1987-1988— © 1987 Graded Press; "Shrove Tuesday Pancake Supper"—Spring 1988— © 1987 Graded Press; "Easter Lilies"—Spring 1992— © 1992 Cokesbury; "All Natural Easter Egg Hunt"—MAM 1994— © 1993 Cokesbury; "Custom-Made Easter basket Service"—Spring 1988— © 1987 Graded Press; "Mother's Day"—MAM 1993— © 1992 Cokesbury; "Host a Mother's or Father's Day Banquet" (adapted)—MAM 1994— © 1993 Cokesbury; "Fall Festival"—SON 1991 ("Halloween Maze")— © 1991 Graded Press; "Halloween Prank

95 96 97 98 99 00 01 02 03 04 — 10 9 8 7 6 5 4 3 2 1

MANUFACTURED IN THE UNITED STATES OF AMERICA

CONTENTS

INTRODUCTION

This is a book about how youth can raise money for their causes. It assumes that young people care and want to raise money for things that count. Since you picked up this book, you must be a carer and a fundraiser! The question is, What do you care about and raise funds for? Most youth groups raise money for lots of things:

- cool programs, retreats, or events
- expenses for mission projects or work camps
- special mission funds
- support for the local church
- fun trips
- ongoing budget needs.

More things could be added, but this list covers what seem to me to be most important. I hope your youth group is raising money for at least some of the first three or four items. If you are not working hard on a cause beyond your own group, you need to be! Chapter 1 tells why!

If you are a youth, you will notice that this book is addressed directly to you. These are fundraisers for causes. If you want the youth in your church to experience ownership and responsibility for what they work on, youth and adults must work together to plan and make decisions. This does not mean that adults wash their hands of your projects. Far from it! What it does mean is that there is an exciting mutuality in your combined efforts that allows

amazing things to happen—and scary things, too, sometimes, with bumps along the way. But we learn from the bumps as well as from the successes—and it's an awesome and enabling process! Speaking of bumps, I get goose bumps just thinking about it!

Now to give credit to the youth and adults who have contributed ideas to this collection. Many of the fundraisers have come from the pages of *Direction in Faith*. Others come from ideas I've jotted down on bits of paper at youth events or gleaned from idea sheets and resources given to me by youth and by adults who work with youth. I thank you all. This collection comes from our common efforts. The ideas presented here probably will stimulate spin-offs and still more fresh new ideas. For now though, let us "keep on keeping on" with our work for peace, justice, faith, and the bringing of God's community to our world.

Happy Fundraising!

CHAPTER ONE

"Doin' the God Thang"

ARE YOUR FUNDRAISERS GOING WHERE THEY SHOULD?

I read about a youth group that changed radically while the young people were scouring harvested fields for leftover fruits and vegetables for the poor. In the middle of that sweaty, exhausting work, they heard God call them. They felt led to do more for and with poor and disadvantaged people. Instead of doing occasional mission projects, they started doing something every month. They kept a scrapbook of their projects and had T-shirts made. The shirts said, *"Doin' the God Thang! —Little children, let us love, not in word or speech, but in truth and action (1 John 3:18)."* They began to "walk the talk" of their faith in new ways.

WALKING THE TALK

Your youth group can use this book for many things. You can use it to raise money for spiritual life retreats, speakers' fees for special programs, pizza, ski trips, and travel to big youth gatherings that can change your lives. You can raise money to buy new furniture for the youth room or to pay for singers for a Christian rock concert. There are many important things to raise money for in a good youth ministry program. The question is, are you doing enough for *others?*

The church is filled with people who think that being a Christian has to do only with believing in Jesus, avoiding certain sins, or developing a good spiritual life. But Jesus was clear that it is more than that. Talk is easy. Jesus told us to "walk the talk" of love.

In John 21:15-17, Jesus asked Peter three times whether he loved him. Each time, Peter answered basically the same thing: "Of course I love you, Lord!" And every time Peter said that he loved him, Jesus replied, "Then feed my sheep." Three times. "Read my lips. Do you love me? Then DO something for my hurting children."

The message is the same for us! "Kim, do you love me?"

"Yes, Lord, you know that I love you. Don't I go to church every Sunday? Am I not almost always at youth meetings? Don't I usher in church? Don't I pray every night?"

"Then feed my lambs, Kim."

"Feed my lambs, Juan Carlos."

"Feed my lambs, Chris."

That is how Jesus responds to the declaration of love. What

Love Notes

Study **John 21:15-17**—and the Scriptures listed below—in your youth group. Divide into small groups and discuss the message you hear. Then come back together to share each group's insights.

♥ **Matthew 25** (in as much as you have/haven't given to the least of these, you have/haven't given to me)
♥ **Matthew 6:19-21** (where your treasure is, there will your heart be)
♥ **Deuteronomy 5:6** (place no other gods before me)
♥ **Matthew 19: 16-22** (the rich young ruler was a good guy, but could not give up his "stuff")
♥ **James 2:14-17** (praying for the hungry without doing something for their physical needs is not good enough)

What does "the God thang" mean to you?

do *you* do with that declaration? The youth group at the beginning of the chapter felt God leading them to make changes. Are there new ways in which God might be leading you? You will find some suggestions in this chapter to help you answer that question. A heart appears beside each suggestion.

CHECKUP TIME

When we listen seriously to God's Word, most of us feel led to do more. We *want* to give more of ourselves, our talents, and our money. It's just that there are so many other things that crowd in. And often they are *good* things. Do you remember the Commandment that says not to put any other gods before God? Of course we do not worship any idols, but it may be more complicated than that! Read the questions in this box. **First, ask them of yourself. Then think about them in terms of your youth group as a whole.**

Love Notes

Are there things you put "before God"? (Be honest!)
♥ Where does your money go? (How much goes for concerts, snacks, recreation, clothes, CDs? For meals, gasoline, expenses for yourself? For God and God's people?)
♥ How is your time used?
♥ Does God get the leftovers?

The next question is "how much?" You can answer that after you decide whether to give your leftovers or give off the top. Try the adventure of giving out of *"your"* stuff, not just leftovers. You might begin by giving up a soda once a week and donating the money to a God Cause. Or you might take the ultimate challenge of giving a percentage of your income. The Bible says that we should give at least 10 percent of what we have. That means giving 10¢ out of every dollar and keeping 90¢ for our own causes. Think about it! Would you be willing to make a pact with God and "pledge" a certain percentage of your money? What about your time?

CHALLENGE

After you compare what you believe God *wants* you to do with what you *are* doing, you are ready to decide where to go from here. Honestly realize that there is more "brokenness" in the world than you can fix. Do you still want to pick up Jesus' challenge, or does that realization make you choose to leave it? Do you choose to reach out to brothers and sisters in the world who are hurting, or to ignore them and concentrate on yourself? Is it worth trying? The parable in the box answers part of that last question for me.

It is the same with us. We are called to feed God's sheep one at a time—and to work to change things at the root level—systemically, socially, economically, politically, and spiritually. We are not called to change the whole world, though the world gradually will change as more of us do our small parts. We are called to be faithful, to try, to do what we can. The choice is ours. I hope we choose to do more and more . . . of "God's thang."

Love Notes

Read and discuss with your group.

A man was walking along a beach early one morning when he saw a young man in the distance. As he watched, he saw the young man reach down, pick something up, and heave it as far as he could out into the ocean. Again and again he did it. As the older man came closer, he saw what the boy was throwing. He was throwing starfish! The man was curious and walked toward him. Soon he was close enough to talk, and he asked the boy what he was doing. "All these starfish washed onto the shore during high tide," the young man replied, gesturing to hundreds of starfish strewn on the beach. "I'm throwing them back into the ocean so they won't die." The older man smiled. "That's a nice gesture—but it's useless. Do you know how many starfish all over the world washed up last night? Probably millions! It's nature's way of thinning the crop. And besides, there are so many, you can't make any difference." The young man bent over and picked up another starfish. He hurled it as far as he could into the waves and turned to the older man. "I made a difference to that one," he said simply.

Love Notes

1. Ask everyone in your youth group to write, draw a picture, or talk about what "thangs" they believe God wants them, as individuals, to do for other people. Give people who feel comfortable doing it a time to share—in two's and three's, or with the whole group.

2. Then discuss **what you** as a group **feel led to do**. (This will affect your Master Plan in chapter 2.)

HOW TO GIVE

For people who want to help others, there are at least two important ways to be in service. Try to build both kinds into your mission strategy.

FIRST, plan to help people on a person-to-person basis. In "hands-on" projects, you give of yourself—though you often will need to raise money for expenses, too. Sometimes you might go on a big mission trip or to a work camp in another place. Most of the time, however, you will be helping people in your own congregation, school, and community. Plan hands-on projects regularly throughout the year. Decide how often you want to serve, follow your master plan, then reevaluate in a few months. An excellent book to help you develop your mission plan is *Beyond Leaf Raking: Learning to Serve/Serving to Learn* by Peter L. Benson and Eugene C. Roehlkepartain (Nashville: Abingdon Press, 1993).

SECOND, plan to give to churches and connectional mission funds. These are funds in which you "connect," or combine your money with other people's money, in order to help people who cannot be reached through hands-on projects, and to help people to help themselves. Without help from connectional mission funds, those people would "fall through the cracks."

Many denominations have their own connectional funds. For example, United Methodist youth have their own mission fund. Called the Youth Service Fund (YSF), teenagers from across the United States raise money that goes to help youth all over the world. Youth in the Evangelical Lutheran Church in Canada raise money for the

NONDENOMINATIONAL MISSION FUNDS

There are a large number of nondenominational funds that help people around the world. Here are two of them.

United Nations International Children's Emergency Fund (UNICEF)
333 East 38th Street
New York, New York 10016

CODEL, Inc.
Room 1842
475 Riverside Drive
New York, New York 10115

National Youth Project, and youth in the Assemblies of God Church raise money for Speed the Light. Check with your own church denomination or organization to see if there is a fund you can support. Or there may be agencies in your own community you would like to support.

Love Notes

Talk about the two different kinds of helping. Then try "The Balloon Game" for a fun way to see why raising money for connectional missions should be an important part of your mission plan! Plan to raise money for connectional mission work every year—or pledge a percentage of all your fundraisers. Individual youth may want to pledge some of their money to connectional missions, too. Decide how much to give and put it in your Master Plan!

The important thing is to do it!

CONCLUSION

I said in the introduction that the fact that you picked up this book shows you care—and that you raise money for what you care about! Reading this chapter shows that you care about a lot more than just yourself and your own friends. It shows that you care about people you do not even know. You care about "walking the talk" and "doin' the God thang." You care a lot!

The options are yours, and you have a world full of them. It is up to you to decide which paths to take. Work with your youth group to develop a Master Plan. Figure out how much money you need and how you plan to raise it. Plan well. Work hard. And have great fun—raising money that ultimately "counts."

THE BALLOON GAME

This raucous "game" helps youth groups visualize why connectional mission funds are important. The game itself is actually sort of crazy! The understandings come as you set it up before you play and debrief afterward.

STEP 1: Give everyone two balloons and a marker.

The balloons represent real-life persons in need. Take a minute to brainstorm some of the needs people have. Draw faces on the balloon people, decide where they live, give them a name, and think about what needs they might have.

STEP 2: Divide the group into four segments.

Each group represents a different type of youth group. Tell each group what kind of group they are. (Which group do you think should have the most and which the least?)

#1 Group: Fun and Fellowship Type. The youth in this group care about each other and come together primarily to have a good time and enjoy each other's company. They do no missional work.

#2 Group: Fun + Spiritual Type. These youth care about each other and have fun just like the #1's do. They also concentrate on developing their spirituality.

#3 Group: Fun + Spiritual + Hands-On Mission Type. They do the same things the first two groups do. They also help other people in person-to-person mission projects.

#4 Group: Fun + Spiritual + Hands-On Mission + Connectional Mission Type. These youth combine all of the above qualities and add one more. They

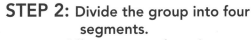

contribute to connectional mission funds. They give their money to help needy people all over the world.

STEP 3: Prepare everyone for the next step!

Tell them that in a minute everyone is going to hold their balloon people over their heads. When a signal is given, they are to drop them. When that happens each group will handle these falling "people" differently.

#1 Group: The Fun and Fellowship Group will be oblivious to the balloons falling around them. They will keep going around the circle high-fiving each other and "having a good time!"

#2 Group: The Fun + Spiritual Group will be genuinely concerned about each other and go around their circle patting each other on the back. They will do nothing about the balloons falling around them either.

#3 Group: The Fun + Spiritual + Hands-On Mission Group will work hard to keep their balloons in the air. But since they only do hands-on mission work, they can deal only with their own balloons in their own place in the room.

#4 Group: The Fun + Spiritual + Hands-On Mission + Connectional Mission Group is involved in hands-on mission work *and* in supporting people in many other places. They will try to keep up *all* the balloons in the room.

STEP 4: Give the signal and see what happens!

STEP 5: After a minute or two, stop the activity and debrief.

Ask questions. What observations do participants have? Did they think about the balloon people while they were playing the game? What about now? Where are you now in real life? Are you satisfied with where you are? What could we do to see that more people are helped

CHAPTER TWO

Laying the Foundation

MAKE YOUR FUNDRAISING MORE SUCCESSFUL

Have you noticed that builders always lay a foundation before they start building? They never say, "Hey! Let's build a house today and forget the foundation!" Why not? Without a foundation, it would not work!

Fundraising is the same. If you want your fundraising to be successful, you need to lay a foundation. If you want to raise a lot of money, you need to set goals, make a plan, and have lots of publicity.

I once saw a cartoon that showed a sad-looking little guy gazing at a sign that said, "Mood Clinic. Hours: Anytime we feel like it." Some youth groups raise money that way—sort of haphazardly and without a plan. If your group falls into that category, you can turn things around. Youth groups always need to raise money. Here's a blueprint to make your fundraising more effective!

STEP I: DECIDE "WHAT FOR" AND "HOW MUCH"

There is more to fundraising than getting money for the group. It is a way for everyone to work together for a common cause. Fundraising done well can build fellowship, unity, leadership skills, and a strong sense of purpose beyond yourselves.

First, the group members need to decide what programs, retreats, work trips, and mission projects they want to do for the next six to twelve months. After that part of the Master Plan is in place, you need to estimate how much the entire plan will cost. This could be done by the whole group or by a small committee. (See the sample plan at the end of the chapter.) Developing a cost estimate lets you see how much money needs to be raised to support the plan. The next step is to decide:

1. how much you need to raise with fundraisers;
2. how much should come from your own personal giving.

("Checkup Time," in chapter 1, shows how to determine this.)

WHAT TO DO? WHAT TO DO? WHAT TO DO? WHAT TO DO? WHAT TO DO? WHAT TO DO?

STEP II: DEVELOP A PLAN

Now you know about how much money you need from pledges and how much from fundraisers. Use that information and the ideas in this book to plan which fundraisers you want to do for the next six months to a year. As you select fundraisers, limit the number of big fancy ones to one or two a year, or else you will spend all your time raising money! Also plan a variety of types and stick mostly with fundraisers that offer good value for the money.

When you have planned *which* fundraisers you are going to do and *when* you are going to do them, go ahead and put them on your group's calendar. For things that use church facilities and involve the whole congregation, clear the event with the church office now. If other facilities or groups will be involved, clear the events with them as well.

MAKING IT HAPPEN

Congratulations! You have dug the hole for the foundation! Now it is time to pour the concrete. Here comes the "nitty-gritty" how-to for making each fundraiser a whopping success.

1. START GETTING READY THREE MONTHS IN ADVANCE. When you put the fundraisers on the calendar in the preceding step, put something else there too. Three months in advance of each fundraiser, put "Plan Crepe Dinner" (or whatever the fundraiser is) on the calendar for your planning meeting. This planning could be done by the leadership team or by the entire group. In that meeting, you need to decide:

- who will do what;
- when things need to be done.

Designate one responsible youth and one responsible adult to make sure everyone is "on track"! (The planning sheet in the Appendix should help.)

WHY? **?????** **?????**

2. EDUCATE AND MOTIVATE! If you want people to support your fundraiser, they need to understand what you are raising money for and why they should give. THIS IS

VITAL! Start your publicity several weeks beforehand—and include those two points. You might even include occasional quotations from your members about what the youth group means to them or why the mission project is so important. If you are in a local church, announce your fundraiser and promote what you are raising money for during the announcements in worship, in Sunday school classes, and at social gatherings. If you are raising funds at a youth event, make frequent announcements in front of the group.

No matter where you are, make the announcements creative—brief skits or role plays about your cause and the fundraiser. Make them funny and/or pointed. Make posters, write articles, and put fun advertisements in newsletters. Advertise in the bulletins for several weeks. If you will be selling things on a certain day, *tell people to bring money!* Put signs on people's backs and fronts for "human sign boards"! As the fundraising progresses, give updates about how far you are toward your goal. Do things with flair and enthusiasm. *Pair the fundraiser and its purpose in everything you do!*

3. EVALUATE! After the fundraiser is over, fill in the section "Ideas for Next Time" at the bottom of the Planning Sheet in the Appendix. You might write, "Fantastic!" or "Never again!" You also might write what worked well and what would have made it better. Keep these sheets in a folder, and you will have an awesome resource for the future—one that can be handed down from one group to the next!

4. EXPRESS APPRECIATION! Thank the people who supported you. Write thank-you notes, put a thank-you letter in the newsletter, make a thank-you poster signed by the whole group, or make a thank-you announcement. If you are using a fundraiser from chapter 8, give the donors a receipt with a thank-you built into it. (Receipts may help for tax purposes.) Make people feel good about their contribution to the cause. It will pay off next time . . . *and* it is a nice thing to do!

5. DEDICATE. When you have all the necessary money in hand for a special project, have a dedication service. Dedicate the money and yourselves to the project you are undertaking. Claim God's continuing blessings on those who will be directly involved, those who are unable to participate directly, those who worked to raise money, those who donated money, and your ministry.

WHAT'S LOVE GOT TO DO WITH IT?

How we do things is, in some ways, as important as *what* we do. Since we are followers of Jesus, we walk in the way of Love. Look at the list of fundraising guidelines. Use them to get *your* thinking started. Your youth group should develop its own standards. The process gives the whole group ownership, and it is important for each person's faith development.

SUGGESTED GUIDELINES FOR CHRISTIAN FUNDRAISING

1. **Be sensitive to people's safety and feelings.** (Ask yourself if there is any risk of anyone being hurt, either physically or emotionally.)

2. **Be sensitive to the language you use.** (For example, say "Service Day" rather than "Slave Day." Slavery is not an issue to make light of.)

3. **Respect God's creation.** (Fundraisers should not be destructive or waste resources like food.)

4. **Be sensitive to the feelings and fears of animals in God's creation.** (Do not use your power over them for laughs—at their expense.)

5. **Avoid fundraisers with a gambling component—like raffles.** (Many churches and denominations have policies against gambling.)

6. **Be inclusive.** (Be sure no individual or group of people is left out or made fun of.)

7. **In all things, act as followers of Jesus.**

USING THIS BOOK

This book is intended for your use. Feel free to modify any of the suggestions to fit your needs. Some of the fundraising ideas are clearly more suited to a local church setting, some to a large group event, and some can be used either way. Be sensitive to what would work best in your own setting and create ways you might adapt! Give fundraisers zappy names, offer home deliveries, and mix 'n match fundraisers—for example, mix a food fundraiser with a special event. Whenever possible, extend your fundraising to neighbors, friends, and local businesses.

As a general rule of thumb, try to provide a high-quality product or service in everything you do—and deliver it with friendliness and appreciation. At youth gatherings, "crazy" fundraisers that provide more fun than value evoke huge amounts of enthusiasm. Among your adult constituency, however, it is best to keep those fundraisers to a minimum—like one a year or so.

Another good principle to follow is variety. Try to make every fundraiser you put on during a year entirely different from the others. For instance, you could plan one Special Event, provide one service, hold one sale, and offer one fundraiser that requires donations. And keep on selling the "cause" as well as the product!

If you work together as a team and follow these principles, your fundraising should be very effective. And you will become a model for the rest of the church in the process.

MASTER PLAN

DATE: _____ **TO** _____

✔ HOW MUCH WE EXPECT TO SPEND:
On a separate sheet, estimate how much things will cost.

STEP 1:
Special expenses
- Service projects
- Planning retreats
- Program retreats
- Mission trips
- Fun trips, etc.

What	How Much
_____	_____
_____	_____
_____	_____
_____	_____
TOTAL	$ _____

STEP 3: Total Expected Expense
(Special & ongoing)

TOTAL $ _____

STEP 2: Ongoing expenses

What	How Much
• Planning retreats	_____
• Curriculum, program materials	_____
• Refreshments, meeting expenses	_____
• Publicity	_____
• Parties, recreation	_____
• Youth week	_____
• Contributions to church	_____
• Contributions to connectional missions	_____
• Leadership training (youth & adult)	_____
_____	_____
_____	_____
_____	_____
TOTAL	$ _____

✔ HOW MUCH WE EXPECT TO RECEIVE:

STEP 4: From outside youth group

Source	How much
_____	_____
_____	_____
_____	_____
TOTAL	$ _____

STEP 6:

TOTAL EXPECTED EXPENSE $ _____

TOTAL EXPECTED INCOME – $ _____

(Add steps 4 & 5 for total expected income. For balance, subtract total expected income from total expected expense.)

STEP 5: From youth group

Source	How much
• Pledges	_____
• Fundraisers	_____
_____	_____
_____	_____
TOTAL	$ _____

✔ BALANCE TO BE RAISED BY YOUTH:

TOTAL $ _____

Delicious Delectables

CHAPTER THREE

SELLING GOOD FOOD IS A GREAT WAY TO RAISE MONEY

Food is a great fundraiser. Everybody likes it, and it has the advantage of giving people something for their money. Only your imagination and your time will limit the possibilities, but some ideas are definitely more profitable than others. For instance, Thanksgiving dinners with turkey and all the trimmings are wonderful but do not provide much profit. On the other hand, a spaghetti dinner or pancake breakfast is almost pure profit.

If you are planning a meal, here is a basic plan:

✔ Plan creative publicity with at least three weeks of lead-in time, using the principles in chapter 2. Select people to coordinate the publicity.

✔ Enlist the help of someone who knows food prices to help plan the menu and set prices.

✔ Sell tickets in advance, but have enough food available for walk-ins.

✔ Decide who will prepare the food, set up the room, wash dishes, and clean up afterward. For jobs that are less fun (like dish washing), consider rotating shifts of workers, so that no one gets stuck doing only dirty work. Work out a schedule ahead of time. Get extra volunteers if necessary. Include at least one or two people who have had experience with preparing large-group meals.

✔ Decorate the area attractively. Think of a theme and coordinate decorations, publicity, dress, and entertainment. (See if there is someone in your church who can get food and accessories at cost, or look in the yellow pages under "Food Products" for discount stores or warehouses.)

✔ Provide musical entertainment if possible. This can be tapes, CDs, a D.J., live musicians who are members of your church or organization, or a band willing to volunteer its services for a good cause, a meal, and exposure. Match the music to the "mood" of the dinner.

✔ Have members of the youth group act as servers. One or two people can function as hosts, warmly welcoming and seating people as they arrive, just as in a restaurant. Show them the youth version of Christian hospitality!

✔ Assign individual youth to wait on particular tables. Waiters provide refills on beverages and clean the tables after each meal.

Love Notes

In every fundraiser that involves food, keep in mind the people who struggle with weight problems, have sugar diabetes, or need heart-healthy low-fat food. Be creative and try to include healthy choices whenever possible.

Coffee Treats Many congregations like to drink coffee and visit between Sunday school and church. If your congregation is one of these, here's your chance to make some good money on an ongoing basis. Secure permission from the church to provide a doughnut/bagel service on Sunday mornings. Poll adults' classes to see how many bagels, doughnuts, or other sweet rolls you might sell on any given Sunday.

If at present there are no drinks or snacks available, ask about interest in beverages, too — and consider providing orange juice as an option. Make arrangements with a local doughnut shop or the bakery at a nearby grocery to have things ready for you early Sunday morning. They may even give you day-old goodies free or at a reduced price.

You will need at least one person to pick up the donuts and juice, and several to make coffee (some adult classes prefer to make their own) and handle the selling. If your church has an early service, be sure you do not interfere with worship. And be sure you finish selling and clean up in time to get to worship!

Bake Sale As long as there is a sweet tooth in America, there will be a market for home-baked goodies. Your youth group can sweeten your treasury and have a lot of fun in the bargain. You need to plan ahead in three areas—advertising, baking, and selling.

ADVERTISING — Begin at least three weeks before the event to put notices in the church newspaper and bulletin, the local newspaper, and other media in the community. Give an announcement to your local radio station at least one week in advance.

Put posters in store windows and other prominent places in town (always with permission). Notices should include place, date, time, the name of your group, and the cause for which the money will be used (mission project, ski trip, or whatever you choose). If you have a special item for sale, be sure it is mentioned prominently. For example, your group may be famous for pecan fudge.

BAKING — Each member of the group may choose to bake an item at home and bring it to the sale. Or you may choose to come together as a group and work jointly on that famous pecan fudge, chocolate chip cookies, or other special recipe. You might even do both.

If members bake individually, try to get some idea about what they will bring so that you can advertise those items. Persuade a few local celebrities (the mayor, the school superintendent, the lady who makes the world's greatest cream pies) to donate their specialties to your sale. Plan to have plenty of special treats on hand.

SELLING — Secure your location well in advance. In county-seat towns, a location on the courthouse square is often popular. In other communities, the best location is at a mall or other shopping area. Remember that you are guests of the people who allow you to use their space. Cooperate with their guidelines and try not to interfere with their regular business.

Some group members need to arrive early on the day of the sale to set up tables. Ask one or two people who are familiar with prices to mark the price on each sale item. Start the sale with an amount of money (small bills and coins) equal to about one-fourth the value of the baked goods you have for sale. Assign specific times to persons who will be selling the goodies. It is important that you have a good time at your sale—fun is as much a reason for a bake sale as money. But don't have so much fun that you forget your customers.

Variations

Look in chapter 5 for seasonal bake-sale ideas, too!

"Other"-Handed Cookie Sale   This cookie sale is like any other cookie sale, except for a special twist. While these cookies ought to taste the same as the usual varieties, they might not *look* the same. Right-handed people are allowed to use only their left hand when they make the cookies, and left-handers can use only their right hand. If a youth encounters a two-handed task, such as tearing open a bag of chocolate chips, that person must ask for help to open the bag! When the cookies are finished, they are to be bagged and delivered in the same manner.

Publicize the "Other-Handed Cookie Sale" in advance and take orders from youth group supporters.

Super Bowl Subs   Making and selling Super Bowl submarine sandwiches to members of the congregation can become a yearly tradition. Fans will appreciate this tasty, easy meal while they are watching the game on television. Take orders at church or by phone for several weeks in advance. Give a discount for prepayments.

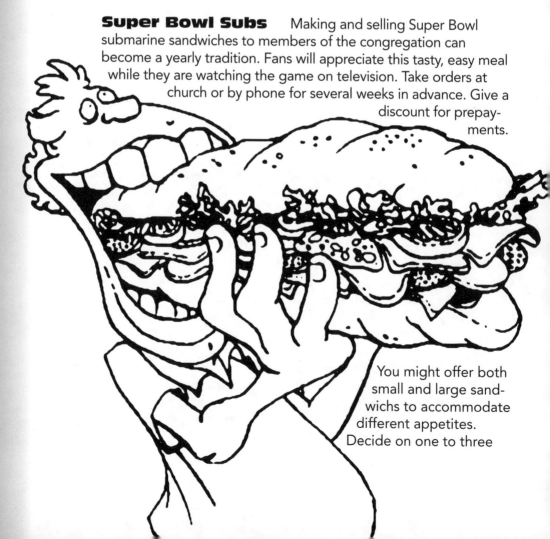

You might offer both small and large sand- wichs to accommodate different appetites. Decide on one to three

SUPER BOWL SUPER SUB SALE!

Treat yourself to a superb submarine sandwich made especially for you by the youth of Vine Street Church!

When? Super Bowl Sunday

Where? Vine Street Church members can pick up their subs in Fellowship Hall after church.

Non-members will have subs delivered to their homes after the 11 o'clock worship service.

How much? 1 for $3; 5 for $13

Why?
*It's EASY! (No cooking or restaurant stops)
*They're GOOD! (Only the best ingredients)
*It HELPS! (Proceeds support the mission program of Vine Street youth)

How? Tables will be set up in the foyer January 14 and January 21 to take your orders—or you may preorder with a member of the youth group by January 23.

"Support Vine Street youth! Order NOW!!!"

✂ -

How many?

____ **PIZZA SUB** (ham, salami, provolone cheese, onions, banana peppers, tomatoes, pizza sauce)

____ **ITALIAN SUB** (ham, salami, provolone cheese, onions, banana peppers, tomatoes, Italian dressing)

____ **TURKEY SUB** (turkey, reduced-fat Swiss cheese, onions, banana peppers, tomatoes, mustard)

Pick up at church or Deliver
(circle one)

Name: _____

Amount: $_____

Youth Contact Person: _____

kinds of subs to offer. If you offer a choice, make order blanks to record patrons' choices when they order. Keep a list of orders and prepayments. Base prices on comparable items in a local deli or grocery store, so that you will be competitive. Motivate people to buy more by offering discounts for orders of five or more.

Check with food wholesalers or warehouse stores about buying ingredients, condiments, and plastic wrap or foil at quantity discount prices. Merchants in your congregation may be willing to donate some of these items.

Some suggested ingredients:

- bologna
- salami
- ham
- turkey
- American cheese
- provolone cheese
- Swiss cheese
- white sub buns

- salt
- pepper
- olives
- tomatoes
- green peppers
- banana peppers
- lettuce
- whole-wheat buns

- onions
- salad oil
- mustard
- mayonnaise
- pizza sauce
- Italian dressing
- pickles

To simplify collections, ask for prepayment on orders from friends and neighbors outside the church.

You should gather early Super Bowl Sunday morning to prepare the sandwiches. (Arrive early enough so you do not miss the worship service.) Make quality sandwiches to ensure repeat business. For instance, you might use 1½ ounces each of two meats and a cheese, add onion slices, banana peppers, and two tomato slices. Use pizza sauce for pizza subs, or give packets of Italian dressing for Italian subs.

> **Mix 'n Matchers**
> A Sub Sale is a great "Mix 'n Matcher"! Have it after church on Sunday, or combine it with a Special Event or Holiday fundraiser. Add drinks, cookies, chips, and fruit, and—bingo!—instant "EVENT"!

Make plenty of extra sandwiches for impulse buyers. Wrap the sandwiches securely to ensure freshness, and keep them refrigerated or in coolers for safety. Church members can pick up sandwiches after church. You will need to deliver orders received from friends and neighbors outside the church.

Have your own "Sub and Super Bowl Party" after all the outside orders have been delivered!

Great Cake Tasting Party
This is a fundraiser that works especially well after a Sunday evening service.

In advance, solicit some "great cakes" and their recipes from church members and friends. Collect the recipes a few days ahead of time and make several copies of each one. When the cakes are delivered, place them on long tables—each cake with its own stack of recipes. Station one or two people behind each cake to cut (into small pieces) and serve. Each patron gets a taste of as many cakes as he or she wants to try. A patron may also ask for and receive recipes. (It might be wise to limit the number of recipes each patron may have, depending on the cost of copies.) Have hot coffee and ice water available.

Charge **a very reasonable** admission. The only expense will be the cost of recipe copies, and perhaps napkins and paper plates, if they are not furnished by the church. Ask one person to donate coffee, cream, and sugar, in lieu of a cake.

A youth choir, an instrumental group, or soloists can provide entertainment. Make it a fun evening!

Here is a "great cake" to present in the advertising:

Chocolate Cream Torte

- 1 frozen, loaf-shaped pound cake (1 lb.)
- 3/4 cup confectioner's sugar
- 3/8 cup cocoa
- 1 1/2 cups whipping cream
- 1 tablespoon cold coffee

Slice the frozen cake into four lengthwise layers. Beat cream with sugar and cocoa until almost stiff. Add coffee and beat until stiff.

Mix 'n Matchers *Another great "Mix 'n Matcher"! This would be a super addition to one of the Special Events in chapter 4.*

Stack the layers, spreading chocolate cream between each. Cover top and sides with remaining chocolate cream. Chill.

Advertise: *"This great cake will be available for tasting. It is only the beginning of an entire evening of savory sampling!"*

Chocolate Fair   Chocolate cake, chocolate pie, chocolate ice cream, chocolate cookies, chocolate mousse—all the chocolate goodies you can think of are a tasty idea for raising funds.

Plan a *chocolate fair*. Several weeks before the fair, decide on the date, location, and time. Have "chocolateers" (chocolate lovers) prepared to bring in their favorite chocolate dishes.

Once you find a location, design a floor plan. Place the tables in a spacious area. In an inner circle, place several tables and chairs for guests. The chocolate booths can be situated in a larger outer circle.

Several weeks before the fair, advertise in newspapers, make posters, and sell tickets. Each ticket will entitle the holder to taste all the chocolate treats. As guests enter, they can be handed menus that include the floor plan. Arrange for live enter-tainment or recorded music to make the occasion more festive.

When the chocolate dishes arrive, list the entries on a sheet of paper, and make labels for each dish. Enlist two persons to serve each station. Have plenty of plates, spoons, forks, napkins, and wet towels on hand. Have water available for those who are thirsty. You may want to add soft drinks, fruit drinks, coffee or milk.

Stay open as long as the chocolate treats last. Your evening will be so sweet!

Heavenly Sundae/Banana Split Party

Mouths will start to water as soon as the publicity begins on this fundraiser! Purchase giant institutional-size containers of ice cream in the "basic three" flavors: vanilla, chocolate, strawberry. (Get a different flavor if you want to be adventuresome—or add a smaller container of low-fat frozen yogurt or ice milk for patrons who watch their fat intake.) Let your mind run free as you think about toppings! Here are some possibilities:

- hot fudge sauce (include plans for heating)
- caramel sauce
- strawberry preserves
- marshmallow goop
- nuts
- whipped cream
- cherries
- crushed candy bits
- granola
- sliced bananas
- pineapple preserves

If you have a large youth group, decide ahead of time whether you want everyone to stick to the same jobs throughout the event. Some think it is easier that way, and some want to swap out the more and less "fun" jobs. Either way, before the event, know who is responsible for getting the supplies and for setting things up. During the event, group members will need to gather tickets at the door, serve ice cream, replenish supplies (toppings, water, bowls, spoons), collect dirty dishes, and wipe up spills.

It is faster if there is one person per container to scoop out ice cream orders as people come through the line. Place the most selected flavors first, and post a sign that is clearly visible listing the choices, so that people can decide while they wait.

> **Mix 'n Matchers**
>
> Heavenly Sundae/Banana Split Parties are great "Mix 'n Matchers"—and not just with other fundraisers. They are a great way to have intergenerational fellowship after Bible study or vacation church school, and they also work well at big events. They are fun to have, complete with music, after a ball game. Invite your friends from school.

After patrons get their ice cream, let them head to the toppings bar to build their own unique creations. Yummy! Be sure you provide plenty of water—and maybe some coffee. All that sweetness will make people thirsty!

Strawberry Patch   If you are living in a place where strawberries grow, plan a strawberry festival. Eating fresh fruit is one of the best ways to enjoy spring and summer. Give your community an opportunity to pick their own fruit. Celebrate by preparing strawberry dishes and a collection of recipes.

peach & pecan party

This activity requires time and work, but it also can be fun and profitable. The first step is to decide whether you will grow your own strawberries or pick them from a local farmer's crop. Select four work committees: gardeners (or pickers), publicity, hospitality, and sales.

Someone you know may be willing to share a garden plot. Ask around. Once the property is selected, the gardening committee needs to begin work. Find an experienced gardener to supervise the work. You will need to decide on the size of your crop and buy the plants. Members of the committee will prepare, plant, and cultivate the soil until harvest.

As the strawberries ripen, the publicity committee will begin its work. Members can advertise in local newspapers, post fliers in neighborhood businesses, and prepare personal cards of invitation for family and friends. Newspapers may charge a minimal fee for advertising. Fliers can be handwritten or typed and copied. The pastor or youth counselor(s) may be able to help think of ways to publicize the event without cost.

Personalize individual invitations. Use unlined index cards, either 3 X 5 or 5 X 8. Design the cards with crayons, watercolors, or colored markers. Be sure to include information about who, what, when, where, and how much. Price strawberries according to quantities picked: pints, quarts, or gallons.

Next, the hospitality committee will begin its work. Choose some strawberry dishes to prepare. Try strawberry preserves and fresh strawberries with whipped cream. For a special treat, have strawberry shortcake. Design a menu in the shape of a strawberry. List selections and prices.

To complete the day, create a collection of recipes. You might call it "From the Strawberry Patch." Use old favorites such as strawberry shortcake and strawberry ice cream. Be sure to include new recipes also. Hand print or type and copy. Set a sale price and print it on the booklet.

Before the festival, design the serving area. Use outdoor tables and chairs, or scatter picnic tables across the area. Give a souvenir to remember the occasion. Those who enjoy sewing and crafts can make strawberry dolls, pillows, or T-shirts.

The festival idea also can work well with pecans, peaches, and blueberries. Choose fruits that are plentiful in your area. Don't stop with one festival. Make this an annual event.

Chili Cook-Off

When the days get cold, a chili cook-off is just what the doctor ordered! It works great before an evening program on a frosty night, or after church on Sunday. Your outlay of money is low and your profit margin is high.

Get as many people as possible to submit big pots of their own favorite chili for an entry fee, which means their meals are free. Then all you need do is provide crackers, drinks, desserts, and maybe chili toppings like cheese and chopped onions. Line up a panel of judges and decide on the categories for judging—for instance, "Most Likely to Please Your Mother," "Spiciest,"

and "Best All Around." Get someone who

Mix 'n Matchers "Mix 'n Match" with an autumn "Hoe Down" or "Talent Show"—or plan a few games to get people mixing, sharing, and laughing!

really has fun with it to be the announcer. If you have a computer person in the group, you can even make certificates of award!

Crêpe Dinner   This fundraiser requires work, but makes a lot of money if done well. It also provides a very different kind of fellowship from that which people usually experience at church. Costs are low, but you can charge big bucks because it is so classy. The key is *elegance*. Borrow fine china, crystal, and silverware from members. Set up card tables with tablecloths and candles. Provide live, classy music such as a string quartet, violin, harp, piano, or classical guitar. Find musicians who will perform free, if you can. Servers wear black pants or skirts, white shirts, and black ties, and give full and formal service. Guests come "dressed to the hilt." (Be sure they know ahead of time!) Create "mood" in every way possible—even down to garnishes on plates!

Provide three crêpe entrees, from which people may select two. The side items could be wild rice, salad, and roll. For dessert, patrons may choose one of three dessert crêpes. Almost all the work can be done a day in advance—maybe an all-nighter? Ask all those who have a crêpe pan to bring it. (These pans are especially good for dessert crêpes, which should be really thin.) You can get an assembly line going—one person dips the batter into the pan and cooks one side. When that side is cooked, flip the crêpe into the next pan to cook the other side. When crêpes have cooled, stack with wax paper between them

LE CHÂTEAU BON

-ENTREÉS-
(Check two)
Includes salad, wild rice, dinner roll, dessert, and beverage.

{ } *Beef Stroganoff Crêpe*
A tempting blend of choice sirloin strips and thinly sliced mushrooms simmered slowly in a delicious cream sauce.

{ } *Seafood Crêpe*
An enticing combination of delicate seafoods artfully presented with a tangy curried fruit sauce.

{ } **Chicken Crêpe L'Orange**
Succulent bits of tender chicken breast irresistibly combined with a savory orange sauce.

-DESSERTS-
(Check one)

{ } **Praline Delight**
Filled with the finest natural vanilla ice cream and smoth-ered with a warm maple praline and nut topping.

{ } **Grasshopper Crêpe**
A mouth-watering crème de menthe filling blends irre-sistibly with the tempting chocolate of the crêpe.

{ } **Blueberry Bordelaise**
A mouth-watering filling of the finest natural vanilla ice cream covered with a tangy hot blue-berry sauce.

-BEVERAGES-
{ } Iced tea   { } Coffee   { } Hot tea

$12.00

"Fine dining with friends in an atmosphere of elegance"

Name: _____

and refrigerate. When dishing out time arrives, take the crêpes out a few minutes ahead of time, so that they will reach room temperature. The filling will warm them up, and no extra heating is required. For recipes, ask at the local library for recipe books for crêpes.

Have people order ahead of time by checking off what they want on fancy menus. One church that started this tradition charges $12 per person, of which about half is profit. As word spread about the event, more people attended each succeeding dinner, and they were even asked to hold dinners for other groups.

Eco-Dinner

This dinner is a great way to conclude a study on our calling to take care of creation. Choose a simple menu—spaghetti, salad, bread, dessert, and drink—or you might want to have vegetarian lasagna, since there is a negative environmental impact from patterns of extensive meat consumption.

Items brought to be recycled should make up part of the cost of the meal. Check with a local recycling center to find out what they accept, what conditions they require (like no paper with glue), and how much they pay. Decide whether you can handle all recyclable items or only certain ones. Make arrangements to transport the items.

Start publicizing several weeks in advance, so that people can collect a large amount of recyclables. When people bring their items to the dinner, you can dramatically visualize the quantities that are going into our landfills. Take it a step further and project how much is thrown away by our entire population! Do not rely solely on written publicity. Make lively, convincing, personal announcements, too.

An Environmental Evening
Saturday
April 4
6 P.M. - 8 P.M.
St. Mary's Church
Parish Meeting Room
114 8th Street, Laurel, MD

- $4 plus one item to recycle per person
- $12 plus four items to recycle per family of 4

"Down to Earth"

- Someone said we have not inherited the earth from our ancestors but are borrowing it from our children.

- *What kind of future am I creating for my children . . . and grand-children . . . and great grandchildren . . . ?*
How much do I care?

- In the end we will conserve only what we love;
we will love only what we understand;
and we will understand only what we are taught.
—Baba Dioum (Senegal)

LEARN about the environment!
Join a recycling or environment club . . . and READ!!!

Steps Toward Caring for the Earth

Step 1: Lack of Concern
"Blow it off"
Discount the effects of your behavior on the earth and future generations
Don't bother with the inconveniences of "doing something"

Step 2: Beginning to Make a Difference
Take steps that are cheap, quick, easy, noncontroversial
Plant a little sapling
Recycle but maintain your current rate of consumerism
Plan an Earth Day event
Buy a Chesapeake Bay bumper sticker
Clean up litter
Read *50 Simple Things You Can Do to Save the Earth*

Step 3: "Deep Ecology" Approach
• Aim your actions at long-lasting, structural changes—confront power structures that put economic and political gain above concern for creation. • Protect a forest from timbering and tourist abuse. • Boycott single-use snack and beverage containers, make serious lifestyle changes so you do not have so much garbage to deal with in the first place. • Live every single day with love and respect for all people and all creatures, always trying to convince others to do the same. • Refuse to use products that contaminate our underground water supply— including poisonous cleaning products, lawn chemicals, chlorine bleach, harsh laundry detergents, and chemically grown food (buy organic food!). • Put pressure on your county government to provide better recycling services and on local businesses to stop using dispos- able products. • Read *Who Will Tell the People: The Betrayal of American Democracy*, by William Grieder.

"To harm the earth is to heap contempt on its creator." —Chief Seattle

Use what you find out from the recycling center and educate people about how to recycle. Your list could include:

- wash steel cans, rinse aluminum cans;
- remove labels from plastic bottles;
- bring steel cans, aluminum cans, colored glass, clear glass, and plastic in separate bags.

 Create placemats or table placards like those on page 40 to motivate people to recycle. Consider having a speaker—or do some teaching yourselves on what you have found out. Advertise fun awards—who brought the most bags, who brought the most in each category, who got their recyclables from the most places. Be sure you use reusable dishes, not disposables! You might even try using candlelight—to illustrate how nice saving electricity can be!

Taste and Tell Luncheon This is a fun way to introduce people to yummy new dishes and also present a high-profit-margin fundraiser. Plan the event for a time when people can easily attend—a Sunday evening or a Saturday. Decide how many meat dishes, vegetables, salads, breads, and sweets you want to have. Ask youth and adult Sunday school classes, and men's and women's groups to submit copies of their favorite recipes—plus prepare two dishes of their chosen recipe for the "Taste and Tell Luncheon." (Be sure to solicit men's recipes, as well as women's, and send thank-you notes when it is over!)

Get copies of all the groups' recipes far enough in advance so that they can be combined into a little booklet for everyone who attends. On long tables, spread out one of each dish, and use *teaspoons* as serving spoons (remember, this is a *tasting* party!). There should be so many entries that people's plates will be piled high with *teaspoonfuls* of these taste sensations! Keep the second dish of each recipe in the kitchen to bring out when the first one is gone.

> **Mix 'n Matchers** Have this in late November or early December and "Mix 'n Match" with a craft fair, letting people pay a nominal fee for a table to sell their handicrafts.

Set a limit on the number of tickets to be sold. Sell tickets in advance, so you know how much food you will need and how many recipe booklets to prepare. Plan to have a few extra for people who show up at the door.

International Night   Invite people from other countries to tell about their native lands. Feature dishes made from the speakers' countries, and have artifacts and pictures on display. Plan with the speakers ahead of time to make the experience as much fun and as educational as possible. For instance, you could get people warmed up by asking them to guess about interesting customs—"How old do you think people are in my country when we start dating? How old do you think we are when we start studying a different language? Do you think dating is the same?" and so on. Ask speakers if they have any tapes or CDs from their countries to use as background music. Finally, plan to learn songs and play games. Get everyone involved!

Potato Bar   For a meal that tastes yummy and is lots of fun, try this fundraiser! Buy great big baking potatoes (small ones for children), provide *lots* of toppings, bread, drinks, and dessert—and turn people loose to CREATE! Use traditional toppings like cheddar cheese, broccoli, sloppy joe filling, hamburger, bacon bits, ham bits, nacho cheese, margarine and sour cream (include low-fat varieties), ranch and Italian dressings, chives, and salt and pepper. Then think of adventurous toppings like salsa, chili peppers, mushrooms, mushroom soup, diced tomatoes, raw onions, and stir-fried or steamed onions and/or green peppers. Add a big bowl of lettuce chunks, and you can have a salad, too!

To be sure the potatoes cook on the inside, buy a bunch of large galvanized nails to stick in them. *Be sure to wash the nails before you stick them in the potatoes!* After you stick the nails in, wrap the potatoes in foil, and allow them to cook for an hour at 350°F. If the oven at the church or facility is too small, designate those who live nearby to fill their ovens at home with potatoes to bake. Ask an experienced cook to help you

> **Mix 'n Matchers**
> A great "Mix 'n Matcher," the Potato Bar goes well with other fundraisers in the Special Events or Holiday sections. For instance, have a potato bar before your Lip Sync Contest!

ensure that the potatoes are done. Leave the foil on, wrap them in a thick towel, and place them in a box or basket for their trip to the event.

Southern Nights   For an evening of fun, plan a "Southern Night"—or use a theme about another area of the country.

Have good food and good entertainment. Serve dishes from different parts of that state or region. List the unique foods of the area. Ask family, friends, and church members to make contributions. Arrange similar foods together. Position tables for easy traffic flow. Some food suggestions for the South: seafood (shrimp, oysters, croaker, catfish), fried chicken, biscuits, pecan pie, chicken livers, poke salad. Decorate the space festively. Place fresh flowers, magnolia leaves, or hurricane lanterns on each table.

Enlist people to participate in entertainment. Focus on variety. Have poetry readings, storytelling, fashions, dances (for example, the Charleston and the shag), and music. Display regional art (paintings, sketches, basketry, quilts) as well.

Sell tickets for the entire event at least a month in advance. Create a minimarket. If people have items for sale, they are welcome to bring them to market. Organize committees to be responsible for room arrangement, food, talent, and the minimarket. Involve as many people as possible.

Serve homemade ice cream for dessert. Give your guests a southern souvenir to take home: peaches, scuppernongs (wild grapes), or shelled pecans, depending on the time of year. Enjoy!

AND MORE . . .

- Have **Concession Stands** at big meetings, ball games, street festivals, or a youth-group yard sale.
- **Cater simple meals** (spaghetti, chili, soup and salad, beef stew, hamburgers, barbeque, tacos or sloppy joes) for couples club, senior citizens, or other groups that meet regularly.
- Take orders in advance and **sell box lunches** after church or at a big meeting.
- Offer regular **Evenings of Tranquility** for young couples—complete with dinner, candlelight, mood music, and baby-sitting for the evening.
- Sponsor **Pancake Dinners or Breakfasts**.

CHAPTER FOUR

Making Memories

SPECIAL EVENTS MAKE MEMORIES AS WELL AS MONEY

riends and laughter are two of God's special gifts—but sometimes people get too busy to enjoy them. This is especially true of adults. When your youth group plans a Special Event, you offer people an opportunity to have fun and savor time with friends. It's almost "sacred space"! Keep that in mind as you prepare. Here are a few guidelines.

✔ *Clear your event with the church office or other planning body to be sure there are no conflicts.* Then put the event on the master calendar and on the youth calendar.

✔ *Use freebies whenever possible.* Some stores and fast food places donate food and supplies for a good cause. Many doughnut places will give you day-old goodies. Sometimes bands will volunteer to perform free if you pay their expenses—especially if they are members of your denomination or group, need the exposure, or believe in the cause.

✔ *Expand your fundraising possibilities at a special event by selling refreshments or simple meals.*

✔ *Send personal thank-you notes to people who volunteered their time and energy to make your event possible.* Send public thank-you notes, by way of posters or newsletters, to people who supported the event. Let them know how much you raised toward your goal and again mention your cause (see sample in Appendix).

Love Notes

When different generations or different groups will be attending a Special Event, plan ways to get people mixing and laughing together!

Family Fun Night

Get together with a team of adults to plan and supervise a tournament of board games. Set up one room for playing various popular board and card games. Set up a recreation area for those who are not competing. Offer Ping-Pong and other games.

Recruit adult Sunday school classes for the tournament of board games. Charge teams $5.00 for entering. Most classes will consider that almost no charge at all and will be happy to help the youth group raise money by having a good time. If you have enough youth for adequate supervision, you might also have a children's tournament.

Assign one or two people as ticket takers. Charge $1.00 admission for those not on a tournament team. Sell soft drinks, cookies, nachos, and pop-

Love Notes
Be sure to word your advertise-ments so that all the people know they are wel-come at "family" events and no one feels excluded. Remember that people who live by them-selves are family, too!

corn. (Arrange for delivery to teams in the tournament.)

Offer prizes of giant candy kisses, ribbons, donated merchandise, or white elephants. Some members of the congregation may be willing to help by donating prizes.

Lip Sync Contest   Challenge youth and adult Sunday school classes to a lip sync contest. Contestants are to mouth the words of their favorite songs while recorded music is playing.

Set up the stage, create a backdrop, arrange for sound equipment, and play the records or tapes for the contest. Consider videotaping the contest. If the youth group is large, you might decide whether to serve a meal.

Begin advertising the event several weeks in advance. Recruit some well-known adults such as choir members, lay leaders, and the pastor to be the stars of the show. Ask permission to advertise, using the names of both the church members and the singers they choose to imitate—Elvis, the Beach Boys, Kenny and Dolly, the Chipmunks, and any more current ones. Remember that adults will be customers and their tastes in music may be hopelessly out of date. Consider recruiting an adult group to do some of the songs from their youth. Another adult class might accept a challenge to try more modern music.

If you plan to serve a meal, decide on a simple menu that will be appealing to all ages, and then ask for donations of food. (Many older persons will

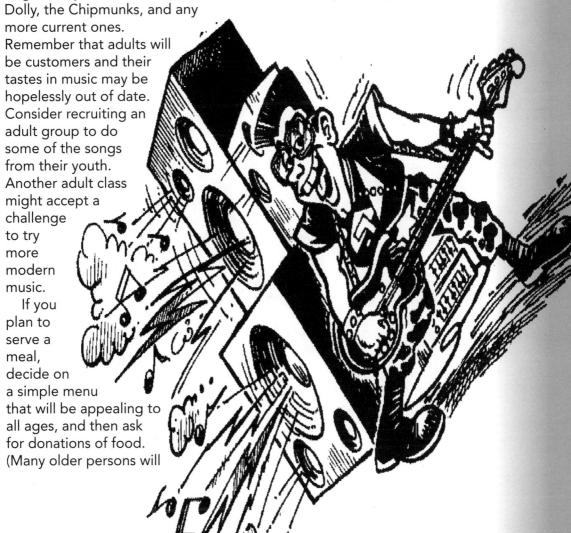

contribute to the youth program by fixing a dish of food.) If you sell tickets or take reservations, you will have a better idea of how much food will be needed. Divide into work crews to set up tables, pour beverages, clear tables, and clean up after the event.

Host a Hoedown!   Country-western has become very popular in the past few years. Host an opportunity for the members of your church, other youth groups, and friends to come and have a country good time!

The evening can include live music or recorded music. Be sure to include some songs that everyone can participate in, such as "Cotton-Eye Joe." If there is a square-dance club in your area, invite the members to come and join in the fun.

Plan a menu of barbeque and cold drinks. You might ask the men or women of your church to host this part of the event. Or you might find a wholesale store that sells ready-made bulk quantities of barbeque and slaw.

Have events for young children, such as a cow-coloring contest or a hog-calling contest. You might also have organized games for the children.

YEE-HAAAAAAAA!

Tie this event to the kick-off of your church's fall programs or as an end-of-summer event. You can charge money for the food, a cover charge to enter the event, or take up a love offering at some point during the day. Invite the people attending to wear their western gear to add to the mood.

Celebrity Look-Alike Contest   For lots of laughs, sponsor a celebrity look-alike contest. In large youth gatherings, it is a stitch. In your local church, it is an opportunity to see church members let their hair down and have fun.

Advertise in youth newsletters, announcements, church newsletters, and through posters, bulletin boards, and flyers. Sell tickets in advance and also at the door.

Target certain persons and invite them personally to take part in the contest: youth workers, staff, and prominent church leaders, both lay and clergy. Be sure people realize that the contest is open to all who would like to participate. If the event is in your church, open the invitation to children, youth, and adults.

Contestants imitate well-known persons, such as TV characters, politicians, a youth worker or other minister, or prominent sports figures. If there is time, it is great fun if the contestants sing, lip-sync, or prepare a word or two to say to the audience in character—maybe giving the announcer a leading question to ask!

The contest will be even funnier if some people cross-dress. For example, ask a man who is a good sport to wear a blond wig and other necessary costume articles to look like Dolly Parton. Someone else could dress to look like a famous TV personality or singer. Those who like to dress in funky laces and outlandish jewelry can pretend to be rock stars. Perhaps someone who has access to an elaborate costume would like to dress like an exotic personality. The only restriction is that all impersonations should be presented with Christian sensitivity.

Select a panel of impartial judges to choose the winners. Award ribbons or certificates in various categories, such as *most authentic, most original, most creative,* and *best of show.* Sell refreshments or have a simple meal at the event to increase opportunities for fellowship and profit. (See chapter 3 for food suggestions.)

Treasure Hunt   The evening is a fun time for an adult Sunday school class party. A treasure hunt provides a chance for teams to follow clues around the local area, while trying to beat the other teams back to the starting point and win the prize. The hardest part of this fundraiser is finding people to donate prizes. Decide on a date to hold your treasure hunt and start seeking treasures at least three months before the event.

Prepare ten treasure-hunt clues in advance.

The clues should lead the team members to the next location, where they will find another clue, and eventually lead them back to the starting point.

Participants will pay $5.00 each. Establish teams of five or six, and be sure that all drivers are over 18 years of age. Give the following instructions: *no speeding, the time to return, ten minute penalties if a team calls for help with a clue.* Station someone by the phone to help teams who call in. Provide refreshments for teams who are waiting for the remaining teams to arrive. Award first, second, third, and fourth place prizes, depending on the number of participants and prizes.

Sponsor a Dance!   Have a dance for the youth of the community, an intergenerational group at church, or a large youth gathering. Use records, tapes, or CDs, or find a band that will donate their time to this worthy cause. Select a special theme, such as "The Fifties" or "The Twenties"—and play the music and learn the dances of the era! Or, if you can find a caller, have an old-fashioned barn dance with square dancing or line dancing! You might even have the event in an old barn and feature hot apple cider and bobbing for apples! Charge $1.00 to get in and extra for refreshments.

Good publicity should bring a crowd and a good source of income. Organize well so that patrons have a good experience and will come back for repeat performances! Make it "a neat place to be," with decorations and lots of energy. If the dance is open to youth in the community, a good time for the dance is after a home game. If you are announcing the dance in church or at a large gathering, dress in a costume appropriate to the theme.

World's Largest Pillow Fight

This event is wild and unique! It works well for small groups, as well as very large ones. Advertise well so as to attract a lot of people. The more people you have, the more fun it will be. Tell people to bring pillows and enough money for admission and food. If a lot of people who do not know one another will be present, plan some crowd-breaker games first to get people talking. Plan to tell people how you will use the money raised. If you want other groups to join you in your cause, tell them how to get involved and motivate through a humorous skit.

Develop rules, decide how much to charge, and determine how long each part of the event should last. Plan a high energy and positive way to make sure that participants are *very* clear on the rules and on the consequences for breaking them. Designate several referees and ask any church members or friends who are registered nurses to be there. Plan what you want to do before and after the pillow fight. Do you want people to hang around and talk, dance, have contests, play games? What refreshments do you want to sell?

Tell a local newspaper reporter about the cause the World's Largest Pillow Fight is supporting, and you might even get news coverage!

Festival of Gifts and Talents

Whether singing a song, playing an instrument, giving a humorous reading, reciting poetry, dancing, juggling, lip syncing, presenting skits, or whatever, people love to get up and perform! A Festival of Gifts and Talents provides that opportunity, gives friends a chance to laugh and affirm each other, and makes money for your project or trip!

Begin advertising and lining up acts about six to eight weeks in advance. The publicity should tell people to bring money, since people vote with money after each act. Be clear in your advertising about what cause the event is supporting. If you are having the festival in your local church, ask Sunday school classes to do group acts. If you are planning the festival for a large youth event, ask each youth group to present an act.

Decide how long the festival should last. When people sign up, ask how long their act will take. Then keep a running tally, because you will have to stop accepting acts when you reach your time limit—remember to allow a couple of minutes between acts. Set a deadline for signing up. Build in enough time in your sign-up deadline for stage managers to develop their plans and program designers to type and print programs (optional). In addition to food, set-up, and ticket collecting, you will need to cover several other key jobs:

✔ One or more lively emcees will announce acts and fill time in-between acts. They can write a script that includes introductions of all the acts—and jokes to fill lulls when they run out of things to say!
✔ An adult and several youth will act as stage managers, making sure all the acts are ready to go and everything is on stage at the right time. They need to develop a list of what to do when.
✔ Money collectors will stay busy tabulating the money that is collected to see who wins. Bring a calculator—and coins to change people's dollar bills during intermission.

You might want to award some funny prizes to the top winners: stuffed animals, certificates, or blue/red/white balloons. Wind up with a grand announcement—with great fanfare—of the amount raised for your cause.

Variations

Ask someone to prepare a silly act. If enough money has not been raised, this act will perform and not stop until the goal is met!

A Day in a Theme Park   This event works best with very large groups of churches or organizations over a broad geographical area, like a conference or synod. If you have a large amusement park in your area (Disneyland, Six Flags, King's Dominion, Opryland, etc.), contact the person in charge of group sales to see if the park would sponsor a Family Day for your group and donate $1.00 of the entrance fee to your missional cause. Generally, they significantly lower the entrance fee for you as well, and sometimes offer other incentives!

This requires the involvement of high-level personnel in your denomination, so that there can be coordinated promotion to all the churches in the area. The theme park will probably handle its own publicity, but you may want to supplement it. The amusement park will have a minimum quota of tickets you will have to sell in advance. Remember to put your cause on the tickets! It is possible to make thousands of dollars for your missional cause every year if you handle this well.

Ask park personnel whether they would allow choirs to sing at intervals in the park during the day. If it is okay, you will need to develop an application procedure. The park may even grant free admission to the choirs.

Sports, Anyone?

A good way to get several generations of church members together in a fun activity and fundraiser is to host a tournament. Tournaments are also fun between different youth groups at large youth events. Choose the type of game(s) after carefully considering the time of year, the available facilities, the people involved, and the weather conditions. You could play volleyball, basketball, touch football, softball, tennis, Ping-Pong, bowling, or other team games. You might even have a checkers, chess, or Trivial Pursuit tournament!

After deciding on the type of game, find a location. Then contact the necessary people to issue the challenge and agree on a suitable date.

Invite members of your community and church or organization to participate in the tournament. Set up different levels of competition by age or ability. Charge each participant an entry fee. Buy trophies for each level of competition. Advertise the tournament through church bulletins, newsletters, posters, and announcements. Decide on an admission fee and sell tickets ahead of time. Sell refreshments at the game to raise additional funds. Encourage members of the participating groups who are not actual team members to serve as cheerleaders during the game.

Present trophies after the tournament. They could be gag-type trophies or regular ones. Some groups like to present them at a big dinner after the tournament. If you decide to go the dinner route, sell tickets or request reservations in advance. (Always be prepared for a few drop-ins.) Include the cost of the dinner in the entrance fee for the participants in the tournament.

Many church members can participate in an activity like this if it is well planned, organized, and advertised early, so people can reserve the date on their calendars. In a local church, you could hold these benefit ball games as an ongoing project. The youth group could compete against the women's group one month, the choir the next month, the men's group the next month, and so forth. You will find many possibilities if you continue to change the game and the group you challenge.

AND MORE . . .

- Have a **Nintendo/Pizza All-Nighter** for community youth.
- Sponsor a **Community Lock-In** with a Christian music group.
- At a **Fashion Show,** have "models" of all genders and ages. Develop a script. Work with a local store if you want a really upscale event.
- For a **Dinner Theater,** provide a dinner and put on a play as professionally as possible. If you provide a good meal, nice decorations, excellent service, and an entertaining play, you can charge accordingly.
- At a **Carnival/Circus,** set up booths for games of skill and chance. Give no prizes, or only free or inexpensive ones. Provide face painting, clowns, acrobats, and refreshments. If space permits, have pets as "trained animals." For adults, you might provide opportunities to buy and sell crafts.

CHAPTER FIVE

Happy Holidays

HOLIDAYS OFFER FANTASTIC MONEY-MAKING OPPORTUNITIES

*H*oliday fundraisers that will help people with some of their seasonal tasks—and provide them with a way to support a special cause or interest. Make each fundraiser a tradition from year to year, and your business will grow as your reputation spreads!

Look in chapters 3 and 4 for additional guidelines.

Love Notes

Remember the people who are alone on holidays. Are there ways you can reach out to them?

Valentine Cookies   This project is a special way for parents to send messages to children, friends to friends, children to grandparents or parents, husbands to wives, and church members to pastors and Sunday school teachers. In church, for several Sundays before Valentine's Day, take orders from people who want to send valentine cookies to special people. Give three choices of messages for the cookies:

❤ "I Love You"   ❤ "Be Mine"   ❤ "Thanks"

Give customers pieces of red paper cut into a heart shape to write their own personal messages to their valentines. Be sure to find out where to deliver the valentines. Schedule a day before the Sunday the cookies are to be delivered to bake and decorate them. Use a basic sugar-dough recipe. Cut the cookies into four- or five-inch heart shapes, bake, and decorate with the messages. After the frosting is dry, place each cookie in a plastic bag. If you plan to make the cookies several days in advance, you could freeze them. When it is time to deliver the cookies (be sure to allow enough time for thawing if you have frozen them), attach the personal notes with tape to the outside of the bag and deliver.

A Valentine Banquet   This dinner can be lots of fun to put together and lots of fun to attend. Schedule it in your church on or around Valentine's Day. Extra effort will make this evening meal a treat for everyone who attends. Decorate the room with red and white balloons and crepe paper. Use red paper to cover the table and white napkins as accents (or white tablecloth and red napkins). Have red and white candles on the tables. Set up a table with a punch bowl and relishes and dip, or cheese and crackers, for people to eat as they arrive and greet one another.

As people arrive and throughout the evening, have a DJ or live musician play love songs for background music. A guitarist, pianist, harpist, or strolling violinist could serenade the guests. After they are seated, serve a tossed salad. Next, serve a plate of spaghetti and a piece of French bread. After you have cleared the dinner plates, serve vanilla ice cream and heart-shaped cookies. People will appreciate the special treatment and service.

Take reservations for your dinner so that you can prevent buying too much or too little food. Be willing to spend enough money to make a tasty meal. Charge enough money to cover the cost of decorations, food, and allow for profit.

Singing Valentines   Here is a great way to help people show their appreciation to friends and loved ones on

Singing Valentines
For Sweeties . . . and Friends

♥ **Show someone you care . . .**
♥ **Do something special and different . . .**
♥ **Send a Singing Valentine!!!**

Choose from four songs:
- "Let Me Call You Sweetheart"
- "I Just Called to Say I Love You"
- "You Are My Sunshine"
- "Friends"

. . . and more options!
- Valentines sung by phone ($3.00)
- Delivered in person ($8.00)
- Add a single rose (an extra $3.00) *(with personally delivered Valentines only)*

Place your order for a Singing Valentine with a member of the youth group by February 10.

Sponsored by the youth of Epworth Church to support their work of helping others.

 -

Yes! I want to order a
singing valentine! (fill one out for each person)

My name is: _____

This is what I want: Telephone Valentine $ _____
In-person Valentine $ _____
Rose $ _____

Total $ _____

Person to receive Singing Valentine and address:

_____

_____

Phone #: _____   (pd/due) [_____]

Valentine's Day. Several weeks before the day, begin to advertise in your church or organization that people can hire your group to deliver singing valentines. If you can handle the business, you may want to advertise also in the community. Decide when you will offer the service and the number of components you will offer. Price each component separately. You can include:

- singing over the phone
- singing in person
- a plate of valentine cookies or banana bread, wrapped in red cellophane
- a gift basket (buy baskets and fill with cheese or low-fat spread, crackers, chocolates, fruit, and a poem—and wrap with red cellophane tied with a big red bow)
- a rose (purchased from an inexpensive discount store)

Think about distances when you set prices and decide what to offer, and set limits for the area you will serve. (You may decide to offer only phone valentines, if the distances you will have to travel are very great.) Next, decide what songs you will offer. Choose some "golden oldies," as well as more modern songs—with something for every generation. You might include a friendship song, too. Practice singing and harmonize, if you can! You might even designate some youth to fall down on their knees and stretch out their hands, for a really dramatic ending!

Collect money when people place their orders, and be sure to get the names, phone numbers, and addresses of the people to receive singing valentines. If customers are ordering a basket, provide a card for them to write a message to include in the basket (make them out of note-sized pieces of paper and seal them with valentine stickers). To avoid traveling in circles when delivering the valentines, have someone who knows the city well plan the route. Plan a "delivery day." Call beforehand to ensure that the recipients are at home. Have all deliverers wear something red or "valentine-ish."

Variations

This is fun at large group events, too. The difference is that songs are sung while people are at the event. Forget the elaborate choices, but you might include a heart-shaped cookie or a candy kiss and a note. If you can "track" people, have a band of minstrels sing to them during breaks. Otherwise, call people up to the stage periodically, and have the singers sing to them there. Ham it up by singing on your knees.

Shrove Tuesday Pancake Supper   This is a good way to raise funds and promote Christian fellowship in your congregation and community. Once you have had a successful pancake supper, you might want to make it an annual event that everyone can look forward to. Your youth group will have an ongoing way to make a healthy profit each year.

Advance planning and good organization are the secrets to success. The following list provides some things you will need to do.

✔ **Secure permission** to use the church kitchen and fellowship hall. Clear the event through the church office to avoid schedule conflicts.

✔ **Advertise** the pancake supper in church bulletins and newsletters, bulletin boards, posters, and flyers for several weeks. Ask the pastor to make an announcement from the pulpit and the teachers to tell their Sunday school classes. If the event is open to the community, plan how to advertise and sell tickets there.

✔ **Sell tickets** in advance. You need to know how many people will attend the supper. The amount you charge will depend upon how elaborate your menu will be. Charge enough to cover expenses and make a profit, but not so much that church families cannot afford it. You probably will want to charge one price for an adult's plate and a lower price for a child's plate.

✔ **Make a list** of all needed equipment, supplies, and groceries. Decide who is responsible for shopping, setting up, cooking, and cleaning.

✔ **Assign specific duties** to each group member. For example, you need people to cook; take tickets; pour coffee, milk, or juice; serve plates; and clear the tables. List in large print on a poster the various tasks and the names of all the people responsible for those tasks. Place the poster where all workers can see it as they work, to avoid questions such as, "Who was supposed to heat the syrup?"

✔ **Have a practice session.** Make pancakes and let the group members enjoy them. Such a session will help you remember what you might have forgotten and also will give you an idea of how much time to allow for cooking, serving, and cleaning.

✔ If your church kitchen does not include a large griddle, **borrow several electric griddles** from church members. Remember that you will need electrical extension cords, coffeepots, mixing bowls, and spatulas. If you plan to serve bacon, sausage, or both, be sure to have an ample supply of skillets.

✔ **You will need these supplies:** pancake ingredients; bacon, sausage, or ham; butter or margarine; syrup and honey; fruit juice, milk, and coffee; cream and sugar; paper plates, paper cups (hot and cold), and napkins; knives, forks, and spoons; tablecloths; tables and chairs; and centerpieces.

PANCAKES

Follow the directions on the back of a box of pancake mix or Bisquick for excellent pancakes, or make them from scratch, using the following recipe.

3 cups flour
4 teaspoons baking powder
1 teaspoon salt
2 tablespoons oil or
   melted shortening

2 cups milk
1 egg
1/4 cup sugar

Mix and sift dry ingredients. Mix egg and milk together, then add oil and stir into dry ingredients, mixing until smooth. Drop batter onto well-greased hot griddles by spoonfuls (or pour from a wide-mouthed pitcher), allowing for spreading. When the pancake is puffed, and bubbles have broken on top, it should be browned evenly on the underside and ready to turn with a spatula.

BACON

If you pan-fry bacon, place the slices in a cold skillet. Heat slowly and turn slices to cook evenly. Drain on a paper towel.

Or you can arrange bacon slices in a large shallow broiling pan and cook three inches below the oven's broiling unit. Turn once to brown evenly.

Bacon also can be baked in a 400-degree oven in a large shallow pan. This method will take about ten minutes.

If your church has a microwave oven, you can cook bacon slices between sheets of paper towels. Allow one minute per slice of bacon in the microwave.

PORK SAUSAGE

Pork sausage links are probably the easiest meat you can cook. Place sausage links in skillet, add a small amount of water, cover, and simmer for five minutes. Drain and pan-fry until brown on all sides. You can buy sausage patties already formed, or form your own patties from bulk pork sausage. Place in cold skillet and cook over low heat twelve to fifteen minutes or until brown. Pour off fat as it gathers, and drain on paper towels.

SPECIAL SYRUPS

• Mix melted butter with maple syrup and warm over a very low heat.
• Mix honey with a small amount of frozen orange juice concentrate. Add a dash of cinnamon and heat before serving.

An Added Touch

To give the pancake supper plate a special appearance as well as taste, add a piece of fruit to each plate. Use warm canned pineapple with a cherry in the middle, canned spiced apple slices, a peach half, or an orange slice. For a neater and more attractive serving, use divided paper plates.

Easter Lilies   The lily is a symbol of resurrection and new life. Many sanctuaries are decorated with lilies on Easter morning. Organize the purchase of Easter lilies by taking orders from members of the church. Order forms should include the name of the giver and the name of the person to or for whom the lily is given. Flowers may be given to honor a living friend or relative, or in memory of someone who has died. The forms also should indicate whether the plants are to be picked up after the Easter service or to be given away. Give the information on the order forms to the church secretary so that the names can be listed in the church bulletin or posted. The lilies should be ordered well ahead of time and delivered on the Saturday before Easter. Arrange the plants in the sanctuary, and designate youth members to deliver unclaimed plants to church members unable to attend Easter services.

Be sure to check with the altar guild or worship committee before you begin this project, since they typically handle special sanctuary decorations.

All Natural Easter Egg Hunt   If your church hosts an Easter Egg Hunt, here's a way to add a new twist to the fun. Make your hunt an **all natural** one. This hunt has several aspects to it.

First, plan on using natural plants and vegetables for dyes. Each child should bring two unboiled eggs. In pots of water, boil red or yellow onion skins (for red or yellow dye), blackberries (for blue dye), spinach leaves (for green dye), and cranberries (for pink dye). When the dyes have reached the desired color, let them cool, then pour each dye through a strainer. Bring the dyes back to a boil and use them to hard boil the eggs the children bring. The children should dip their eggs in vinegar water, write their names or initials on their eggs, and then let an adult or youth boil the eggs (for about 12 minutes). Let the eggs cool before the children touch them.

While the eggs are cooking, send the children on a hunt. Place paper eggs at various locations around your area. Give each child a map to follow to find the eggs. Each egg should have a letter written on it. When the children find an egg, they should write its letter on their sheet of paper (leaving the paper egg where it is). The letters on the eggs should spell out a message, such as "Happy Easter" or "Jesus lives." The number of paper eggs you need to hide will depend on the message you choose.

Along with the egg dying and the hunt, have other activities for the children, such as clowns, puppets, and so on. Make this a festive occasion. Charge a small admission fee for the children. You can easily invite the whole community to join in the fun.

Custom-Made Easter Basket Service   Your youth group can provide a custom-made Easter basket service, to bring joy to children and save busy parents a lot of time and trouble. Work

Custom-Made Easter Basket Order

Customer's Name _____

Address _____

Telephone Number _____

Personalization _____

Type of Basket (check one) Traditional ___ Nutritional ___

Delivery Instructions:

together to decorate eggs, shop for ingredients, and create beautiful baskets.

Be sure to take orders for the Easter baskets ahead of time. Advertise the project through the church bulletin, newsletter, posters, bulletin boards, flyers, announcements from the pulpit, and in Sunday school classes. Charge enough for each basket to make a profit, but no so much that parents will not consider it a good buy. Collect payment for the baskets at the time the customer places the order.

Customize baskets by decorating the eggs with the child's name. Also, attractively print the child's name on a decorative tag for each basket.

Another feature of the custom-made baskets is that the customer will have the choice of a *traditional* basket, which includes candy, or a *nutritional* basket, which includes only healthful items. Some parents do not allow their children to have sugar, so they would welcome a nutritional basket.

Include in the nutritional basket hard-boiled decorated eggs, small boxes of raisins, individually wrapped granola bars, small packages of nuts, sugar-free chewing gum, plastic eggs filled with California mix (dehydrated fruit), an apple, an orange, or other fresh fruit.

Try to purchase baskets, "grass," cellophane, and ribbon wholesale in order to make a better profit. Ask a florist to teach you to make pretty bows for the basket handles.

A sample order form is at top of this page.

Mother's Day Flowers Keep alive the old custom of wearing a flower in honor of one's mother (pink or red if she's living, white if she is deceased) by providing carnations to church members on Mother's Day. In return, ask for a donation to the youth group's projects.

Host a Mother's Day or Father's Day Banquet

Mother's and Father's Days are special days of the year to celebrate the love we have for our parents and the love they share with us. Treat the mothers in your congregation to a special banquet on Mother's Day and the fathers to a special banquet on Father's Day. They will be glad not to have to wait for the long lines at restaurants and will love the individual attention they will receive.

Take reservations for the banquet ahead of time to ensure proper preparation. The cost of the banquet will depend on your menu. Plan to decorate the tables and to prepare and serve the food. The program can be simple, yet meaningful. Let people know ahead of time that everyone who

Mothers and Children

Mothers are God's precious gifts. And so are children. Though the road they travel together is not without bumps and pitfalls, the relationship they share on the journey forges one of the most significant connections two human beings can share. Parent and child. Think about your mutual journey. Recall the bumps, the joys, and the laughs along the way!

Choose some of these questions—or think of others—and have fun sharing memories! (Also feel free not to share out loud but just to ponder in your heart.)

♥ What are "The Stories" about labor and delivery or adoption proceedings? Share the birthday/adoption stories that begin, "This time _____ years ago . . ."

♥ Share some good memories—and/or some funny ones.

♥ Were there times when it was really hard for Mom to continue to GIVE and LOVE—but she did anyway? Moms, were there times your children were able to "be there" for you?

♥ What are your dreams for each other?

"Thank you, God, for Mothers!"

chooses will have a chance to share something special about their mother or father—whether or not the parent is present. You may choose to recognize special mothers or fathers, such as the one with the most children, the newest, or the oldest. Prepare lists of questions to place on a placard at each table. This will encourage conversation and sharing of memories among people at each table. (Note: The questions in the example can be used for fathers also.)

In Memory/Honor of Poetry Booklets

Produce a small booklet of poetry for Mother's Day or Father's Day. Begin a couple of months in advance to find a few poems to include. When you have found several you really like, let the congregation know that people may buy a line of a poem in memory or in honor of their mothers/fathers—or people who are like mothers/fathers to them. Include in the booklet a page that lists the names of all the people for whom lines have been dedicated, along with the name of the person who has made the dedication.

Fall Festival

Over the years, Halloween customs have changed, and in many areas, trick-or-treating is on the decline. Sponsor a Fall Festival for Families—complete with games, goodies, and costumes as a fun option! You might even want to have a simple meal such as hamburgers or hot dogs. Have a costume contest. Encourage people to avoid the old demon/witch focus and move to a more positive orientation.

Start to plan and prepare for the festival in September. Reserve the fellowship hall or a large Sunday school room for Halloween, and for at least one day before Halloween. Advertise for several weeks in the church newsletter, bulletins, or with posters and announcements. The date, time, place, and food and admission prices should be included in all advertisements.

Halloween Prank Insurance

Sell Halloween prank insurance policies that will be effective on Halloween night. Prank insurance does not guarantee that no pranks will be played. It does guarantee that the youth group members will clean soapy windows, pick up

Prank Insurance

This policy entitles:

Name: _____

Address: _____

Phone: _____

to clean up services after the Halloween horrors of smashed pumpkins, toilet paper, rotten eggs, etc.

All claims must be filed by November 1.

toilet paper that is within reach, dispose of smashed pumpkins, or take care of other carefully designated perils characteristic of Halloween night festivities. This insurance should not cover serious vandalism such as broken windows or sand in gas tanks. The insurance should be paid for in advance, and claims must be filed on November 1, when youth are available to work.

Thanksgiving Bake Sale   Everyone enjoys something special to help celebrate a holiday. But often, people are running behind on last minute delicacies. Therefore, a great time for a bake sale is before or after church on a pre-holiday weekend. Everyone has been to a bake sale, so make this one different. Give the sale a festive flair.

Each youth member can sign up to bring a cake, cookies, bread, or pie decorated for the holiday. For example, for Thanksgiving, bring pumpkin bread or pumpkin pie, cupcakes with candy pumpkins on them, a cake with pilgrims or a Thanksgiving prayer on it, and so on. Let your minds run wild!

Announce the sale two or three weeks in advance, so that people can plan to buy their dessert for the holiday weekend at church. Emphasize in your publicity that these desserts are festively decorated and special for this holiday.

Mix 'n Matchers "Mix 'n Match" with Thanksgiving Bake Sale. In your advertising, let people know their choices, and remind them when to bring their money!

Daily Bread   Thanksgiving is a good time to bake and sell bread. To make bread, you will need bread pans, baking spray or margarine, flour, and plastic bags for packaging. You also will also need bread dough, bread mixes, or ingredients for making bread from scratch. Bread dough can be bought freshly made from a bakery or frozen from a grocery store. If you choose to use bread mixes, you also will need eggs, water, oil, and so forth, as indicated on the back of the package.

Depending on the kind of bread the group chooses to make, set aside a whole afternoon or an afternoon and evening for making and packaging bread.

Two or three weeks before Thanksgiving, advertise the bake sale in the church newsletter and in the Sunday morning bulletin. You might even set up a table outside the sanctuary, offer samples of bread to people attending Sunday worship, and take orders. Suggested sale price for each loaf of bread: $2.00. Be sure to make a few extra loaves for impulse buyers!

Candles for "Saints" This fundraiser is held on All Saints Day in memory of loved ones who have died. Plan to have a dinner and a brief, meaningful Ceremony of Lights right after the church service. Make the dinner something easy to manage, like spaghetti. Keep the program simple, and work with adults to develop it. Using your church's worship book and hymnal, find some meaningful poems, songs, and prayers for your program.

Advertise well in advance. Invite the congregation to order candles in memory of loved ones who have died. Purchase some candle-making kits from craft shops and follow the directions. Make the candles that have been ordered, plus several extra. On All Saints Day, arrange them attractively on a table. After dinner, if space permits, gather everyone in a large circle around the candle-covered table. Begin the Ceremony of Lights. At some point, call forward, one at a time, those who have purchased candles. Invite them to share the name of the person they are remembering, make any remarks they care to, and reverently light the candle. When that person returns to the circle, call the next person forward. After all the candles are lighted, read a concluding poem and/or make your final remarks. If there is no further sharing, perhaps sing a chorus and close with prayer. Tell everyone that they may take their candles with them. (See chapters 3 and 4 for more planning hints for the dinner.)

Love Notes

Be sensitive to anyone who may have lost someone and does not have the money to attend. Tell your pastor you will offer the meal and candle as a gift for that person.

Christmas Cookies This is a great help to people who want homemade cookies for Christmas but have no time to bake them. This is where you come in! Select a variety of delicious cookies to sell. Get lots of volunteers to bake 10 or 12 dozen cookies each. Each person should prepare one kind only. Check the local bakery shops for the going price of a pound of cookies. Get boxes to put the cookies in (corsage boxes are pretty reasonable), sandwich bags for people to wear like gloves when they pick up the cookies they choose, and an accurate kitchen scale. Decorate a room for Christmas and have tables set up to display the cookies. Sell them by the pound. With a good location, and if you advertise heavily in your church, area businesses, and community, you should sell a lot. One way to build interest is to make up a few cookies in advance and have pieces of those cookies available for samples one Sunday. Then take orders for the next several weeks before the cookie sale. After the first year, you will not need samples. Your reputation will be all that is needed!

HINT: When you are setting up the scale, put an empty box on the scale and set it at zero. Then when you weigh cookies for customers, they will receive a true pound.

Variations

Also take orders for homemade bread or banana bread. These are healthy alternatives. Present them nicely wrapped in plastic wrap, with a big bow.

Candy Sale   This is similar to the cookie sale. Decide on a yummy kind of candy, get an experienced cook to help you, and plan an overnight candy-making lock-in! Start taking orders several weeks ahead, and make plenty of extra candy. You will need it! As with the cookies, expect these sales to grow each year. I know of one church that sold buckeyes and, within a short time, increased their candy sales from $300 to $1,500!

Poinsettias Sale   In Mexico, the poinsettia is called "Flower of the Holy Night," and people tell the story of a boy who was afraid to go to church on Christmas Eve because he had nothing to give to the Christ Child. He prayed, "I am poor and dare not approach the Child with empty hands," and immediately, a poinsettia sprouted and grew at his feet. He picked the flowers and gave them to the Christ Child. The poinsettia reminds us of the gifts that God gives us. At Christmastime, poinsettias decorate our homes and altars.

Take orders for poinsettias to decorate the church sanctuary. The poinsettias can be given in honor of or in memory of loved ones. (*In honor of* is for the living; *in memory of* is for the deceased.) Prepare order forms that include the name of the person giving the poinsettia, the name of the person to be honored or remembered, and whether the plant will be taken home or given away after Christmas. When completing the forms, be careful to spell names correctly. After all the orders have been taken, give the church secretary a list of the names of people giving the poinsettias and those being honored or remembered, so that the list can be printed in the Sunday bulletin.

Make arrangements with a local florist or supermarket to buy a number of poinsettias at a reasonable price. On the day the plants are purchased or delivered, arrange them in the sanctuary. Assign each person in the group a time to water the plants, and ask several youth members to be available on Christmas Day to deliver unclaimed plants to sick and homebound members of the church.

Variations

Sell the poinsettias also in the community. Go to restaurants before the Christmas season and see if they want to order some for Christmas decorations. Advertise. Ask your friends. Offer delivery service.

Wrapping Service   The Christmas season gives many opportunities to raise funds. One idea is to provide a gift-wrapping service for members of your church and community.

Order an assortment of Christmas wrapping paper, ribbon, bows, and tape from a local paper company. Ask for volunteers from your group to wrap packages for people after school and on Saturdays until Christmas. Set up wrapping stations in the fellowship hall or Sunday school rooms of your church.

Advertise to your congregation and community that during certain hours on designated days before Christmas, your youth group will be wrapping packages for shoppers. As a group, decide how much you will charge. Consider the size of the packages, the cost of the paper and supplies, and prices charged for wrapping at local stores.

On the busiest days just before Christmas,

sell baked goods, coffee, and hot chocolate to people while they wait for their presents to be wrapped. Your group also might want to include a baby-sitting service for shoppers during the same hours you are available for wrapping. Whether you do this will depend on the size of your group and the needs of the people in your area.

The amount of business you have will depend upon the quality of your work and how much you advertise. Be sure to practice wrapping some packages before you open shop. If your group does a good job with this project, you will be in demand every year, and your business will grow.

Singing Christmas-Grams

Here's an exciting way to help the members of your congregation celebrate the Christmas season and share the spirit of the holiday.

Select a date for your youth group to go out Christmas caroling. Several weeks before that date, advertise that the members of your congregation and community can hire the carolers to sing for people to whom they would like to send a special Christmas greeting. They will then give you the names and addresses of the persons who will receive their singing Christmas-grams. You may wish to have them also give you the phone numbers of the recipients, so you can make sure they will be home.

As the carolers arrive at the designated homes, greet the persons to whom you will sing and let them know who sent them a Christmas-gram. Depending upon the size of your congregation, you may need to set aside more than one night to go caroling. Have someone who knows the city well coordinate the route the carolers take, to avoid traveling in circles.

Variations

Give people the option, for an additional charge, of having the carolers deliver a poinsettia. Call around and price poinsettias. Discount stores often offer great prices.

Christmas Sweatshirts

This event will allow the members of your group to work together on a project, learn some of the talents of the members of your congregation or organization, and raise money in the process.

As people are buying presents for Christmas, give them an opportunity to invest in the youth group as well. The idea is to decorate and sell festive T-shirts and sweatshirts.

To do this, ask members of your church who are good at crafts to help with this project. They can direct you as to what types of shirts to buy and what supplies are needed.

Make several shirts ahead of time to show the members of your congregation and community so that they can place orders. Set aside an afternoon or morning, or have an all-nighter for your group to get together to decorate the shirts. Depending on the number of orders you receive, you may need to set aside more than one time to complete this project.

To cut the costs of decorating the shirts, ask your local crafts store to donate any discontinued patterns. You can quite often find supplies on sale, so keep your eyes open. This project will take some work, but the benefits of working together will far outweigh the preparation time. And who knows, you just might have great fun as you work!

Greens and Chili

Introduce the congregation to the Christmas custom, hanging of the greens. Invite members of the congregation to help decorate the church for the Christmas season (hanging the greens), join in a fellowship meal, and worship in a service of hymns and

"Mix 'n Match" with "Family Wreath Making" for an awesome holiday event that can become a tradition—and make lots of money.

Mix 'n Matchers

Scripture readings. Ask your pastor or the worship committee to work with you to plan the evening.

For a fundraiser, prepare and serve a simple chili supper—chili, crackers, and a green gelatin salad. You will have very little last-minute preparation if you make the chili at home, bring it to the church in crockpots; have the gelatin ready to cut and serve. Provide ice cream, toppings, nuts, and whipped cream for do-it-yourself ice-cream sundaes. Instead of charging for the dinner, ask for donations. That way, no one is left out for lack of money—and some people will donate extra amounts.

Family Wreath Making   Making wreaths is a super way for congregations to begin Advent. Wreath making can be a wonderful time of creativity and togetherness, as families and friends, young and old, work together to make masterpieces for their doors. Publicize it well, make the occasion festive—and it may become a tradition!

Well ahead of time, schedule a date with the church office. Get commitments from several members of the congregation to bring big sacks full of holly, magnolia leaves, boxwood clippings, sweetgum balls, pine cones, other types of evergreen clippings, ribbons and bows, or anything else that might go on a wreath. Take orders for wreaths so you will know how many wreath forms to buy at the local craft shop. (As always, buy a few extra.) You also will need sturdy metal pins to attach the greenery to the form. Ask at the craft shop to be sure you get the right kind. Also get a number of bows—and, optionally, some other baubles—for finishing touches.

Figure your cost per wreath. You can either charge a certain amount based on that figure, or let people know the cost and ask for donations. Either way, announce in your publicity what you are raising money for; but mention that if money is a problem, the materials will be your youth group's gift to them. One advantage of asking for donations is that some people will give you more than the actual cost, and those who cannot afford it are not excluded. You can raise significantly more by asking for donations than by charging a set amount, but you also run a risk. Weigh the options carefully and decide. If you have a meal or refreshments, you can combine the two fundraisers and handle them as a package, or treat them as two separate fundraising opportunities. On wreath-making day, decide where to lay out the greens and other things for making the wreaths. You probably will want to spread them out on plastic or paper—on tables, a stage, or the floor. Have enough additional tables or other work areas for people to spread out and make their wreaths. Two or three wreaths can be worked on at a standard rectangular table. Provide Christmas music or organize some carol singing as you work! If you plan to have the wreath-making after a meal, such as the "Greens and Chili" fundraiser, make a few remarks to set the tone before you leave the tables. Read a Christmas poem or tell a legend about how the use of wreaths or evergreens began.

Advent Wreaths   This is very similar to "Family Wreath Making." But instead of making wreaths for the door or wall, families make Advent wreaths. Since Advent wreaths stay inside, the greenery dries out very quickly if it is live. For that reason, it is best to use plastic or silk greenery. Ask members and friends if they have any old greenery they would be willing to donate. Call several discount stores and see if you can find some artificial greenery that is inexpensive or that they would donate. Buy flat styrofoam forms that will sit on a table, and 5 tall candles—3 purple, 1 pink, and 1 white. *(The purple ones are used the first three weeks of Advent, lighting an additional one each week, beginning on Sunday. The pink one is lighted on the fourth Sunday of Advent. The white one is the Christ candle and is lighted on Christmas Day.)*

Advent wreaths are used during Advent and Christmas devotions to help people think about the meaning of the season. Your youth group can either prepare your own devotional material (start well enough in advance), or you can buy daily devotional booklets that are already prepared and inexpensive.

On wreath-making day, set things up the same as in "Family Wreath Making." For your remarks, mention how important it is for us as Christians to keep the "reason for the season" in our thoughts and hearts. Encourage people to have family devotions regularly, including all members of their families, and genuinely worship. You may want to have a wreath already made up, gather everyone around as you light the first candle, and have the first devotion together.

Fresh Greenery Kits

This fundraiser is great for the Christmas holiday season. People love the smell of fresh greenery during Thanksgiving, Christmas, and New Year's Day.

First, find a company that can provide greenery kits (the kits should include fresh greenery and other items needed to create a wreath). Check with your area garden center or nursery. Either take advance orders or estimate the number of greenery kits you can sell and have them on hand. To boost your sales, display a sample wreath made from a greenery kit for people to see and smell.

AND MORE . . .

- Make and sell **Advent Wreath Packets**, complete with greenery, styrofoam form, candles, and devotional booklets.
- Make **Cereal-Snack Mixes** to sell on holidays.
- Sponsor a **Parents' Day Out** the Saturday after Thanksgiving.
- Provide **Halloween Bibleland Tours** and give the children of your community a Christian alternative on Halloween. Transform a large room or series of rooms into a "Bibleland." Encourage attendees to dress in biblical attire. Create a marketplace with artisans, such as a potter, a weaver, a carpenter, and a tentmaker. Have a Palestinian home and a synagogue. Provide settings for a fisherman and a shepherd. Costumed hosts in each area can help out with craft activities, tell stories, lead games played by children of the time, teach songs or dances, and offer biblical foods.

CHAPTER SIX

Service with a Smile

BY PROVIDING NEEDED SERVICES, YOU HELP PEOPLE WHILE RAISING FUNDS

One of the best things about selling services is that you are helping people. Always make your attitude part of the service. A warm smile goes a long way.

Saturday Fun-Days Give children a treat and parents a daytime break! Sponsor regular Saturday afternoon fun-days for the children in your church and their friends. You might even open it up to the neighborhood. Ask for advance reservations, so you know how many to expect. Plan creative games and art activities. Include physical activity. If you occasionally want to show a movie, select only G-rated videos. (Make clear that the cost is for baby-sitting and food. A costly license is required to show movies for profit!) Provide refreshments. If you avoid treats and beverages that contain sugar, the energy level will be more manageable. One of the activities for the older children might even be

Mix 'n Matchers

Have this fundraiser a couple of times between Thanksgiving and Christmas, when parents need to shop. "Mix 'n Match" with "Wrapping Service" in chapter 5. Provide lots of publicity in advance, and be sure you have enough people to watch the children—and to wrap gifts, in a room away from the children.

preparing some healthy treats. Be sure you have a couple of adults working with you, too.

If you decide to offer fun-days on a regular basis, study a book on positive discipline. It will make your experience happier—and prepare you for positive parenting!

To legally show in a church a video intended for home use, contact: Motion Picture Licensing Corporation, P.O. Box 3838, Stamford, CT 16905-0838 (1-800-338-3870). Request a set of guidelines and ask about their group rates. If your church is small, see if they will come down on their fee.

Car Wash   Sponsor a car wash—with a twist. Advertise that the car wash will be "free"—that is, no set fee will be charged for the service—but you will accept donations.

While some people may take advantage of the free offer without making a donation, most probably will contribute more money than the set fee would have amounted to. To ensure the success of this fundraiser, make certain that those who bring their cars in are aware that donations will be going to a good cause.

When preparing for the car wash, remember several things:

✔ Select a place where abundant water is available.
✔ Have plenty of supplies (water hose, rags, tire brushes, detergent, towels, buckets, sponges, glass cleaner, and so on).
✔ Have two vacuum cleaners, so that two people can vacuum the inside of the car at the same time (one on each side). Vacuum cars away from the wash area, to avoid wetting the interiors and the vacuum cleaners. **Avoid driving the cars. If possible, let car owners move their cars from vacuum area to wash area. One dented fender will more than wipe out your profits and do little for public relations.**
✔ If electrical outlets are not conveniently located, take extra-long extension cords.
✔ Have several people available, in order to work fast and wash as many cars as possible.

Variations

Set up a ticket table in advance. Make a big sign that says, "Get your car-wash tickets now! Free or for donation." That way, people who do not come can still donate. You make more money that way! If it rains, reschedule.

- ✔ Widely publicize your free car wash through church bulletins, newsletters, announcements, posters, and flyers.
- ✔ Make a large sign for the car wash area, indicating that your youth group is sponsoring a free car wash. *For "truth in advertising," clearly indicate that donations are accepted.*
- ✔ Return all borrowed equipment and supplies promptly, and leave the wash area clean and orderly.

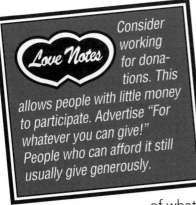

Love Notes Consider working for donations. This allows people with little money to participate. Advertise "For whatever you can give!" People who can afford it still usually give generously.

Rent-a-Kid Advertise for several weeks that there will be an event at which church members and others can "rent" members of the youth group to do certain services—housework, yard work, baby-sitting, and so on. You may want to combine this event with a fundraising luncheon on Sunday or a breakfast on Saturday. In your advertising, give lots of examples of what members of the youth group will be willing to do. Tell parents that they might want to bid on one another's teenagers, rather than on their own.

At the event, have someone outgoing and energetic be the auctioneer, or if possible, secure a professional.

Rent - a -Kid Contract

Jason Adams

Agrees to _cut yard_

of _Dr. Alice Simmons_ on _Sat May 12_ at _12:30 p.m._

Youth
Jason Adams
_555-4482_

Purchaser
Dr. Alice Simmons
823 Orchard St.
_555-9292_

Half the key to success for this fundraiser is getting people to the auction. The other half is having an auctioneer who can work the crowd and prompt people to bid against one another. Fast-paced, competitive bidding is a lot of fun and increases the amount of money made.

Have "Rent-a-Kid" contracts ready to be signed at the event. Both the renter and the worker are to sign the forms and agree on the type of services to be performed, the date for the services to be performed, and the amount of time required.

Sell Your Services   This is similar to "Rent-a-Kid," but has a different twist. Each youth member should decide what services he or she is willing to sell. Sometimes two or three people will want to work together. **For example,** two or three people might offer an afternoon party for a specified number of young children, providing games, refreshments, and so on. Others may offer twirling lessons, swimming lessons, or other skills. Some members may know how to work on cars or bicycles or are knowledgeable about certain school subjects. Others may enjoy working outdoors, baby-sitting, visiting with senior citizens, cooking or baking, caring for animals, or playing musical instruments. Be creative.

Then set a date for an auction. Secure someone to be the auctioneer and another to keep records. Publicize the auction in your community well in advance of the event. Include in the publicity some of the unusual kinds of services you will be offering, as well as the more routine jobs. If possible, get youth leaders, the pastor, and other popular adults to offer services as well. At an auction, the bidding for the pastor to wash a car might go very high indeed! Invite the congregation and community. A church dinner or an ice-cream social would add another dimension to the auction. A large number of people would be at the church already, so a crowd is guaranteed.

As each person's services are sold, he or she should talk with the buyer(s) and make arrangements to perform the services.

Parking   Is your church or facility close to a ball park that doesn't have enough parking space? Make lots of money during home games by letting vehicles pay to park in your lot! Decide on a reasonable rate. Make signs that say **PARKING!** and the amount. Make sure the letters can be seen from a distance (try it out!). Prop the signs on chairs or easels at the entrances to your parking lot—and put one in the church yard, where it can be seen before people get to the entrance.

Collect money as people pull in, and let them park their own cars. Be sure you have an adult, plenty of change, and a money container at each entrance.

Singing Telegrams   Does your group like to sing and get together? If your answer is "yes," you could start an ongoing singing telegram service! You could sing over the telephone or deliver the singing telegrams in person. Decide which you will offer, and on what day or days.

Do you live close enough to each other to make delivery feasible? Divide your group into teams of about four persons who will sing the telegrams when needed. One person should be in charge of taking calls for the telegrams. When someone calls, find out where the recipient lives and send the closest team to that address. After a while, the teams will develop their own style of presenting the telegrams, and church members will request a certain team for a telegram.

Creative members of your group could write several telegrams for birthdays, anniversaries, and other occasions. Or choose an already-written song to go with one or more of the following topics:

- Happy Birthday
- I love you
- I'm sorry
- Have a good day
- I'm glad you're my friend

Variations

1. Sell singing telegrams at large events. They are lots of fun! Have singers seek out the person if the crowd is not too big. Otherwise, the people who have had telegrams bought for them can be called up on stage and sung to in groups. If notes are to be delivered, spread them out on a table and let recipients pick them up on their way back to their seats.

2. If you have the delivery service, decide whether you want to give customers the choice of ordering something to go with the song: a flower from a nearby discount florist, a balloon, or a personal note. If you decide to offer products with your service, have everything on hand that can be stored, and make a step-by-step plan for obtaining the rest of it quickly when you get an order. See if you can arrange discounts with stores.

Practice singing together until you are pretty good. Then advertise the possibilities you are offering! Once the idea catches on, singing telegrams can be a fun, year-round fundraiser that your group will enjoy.

Recycling for Funds   Collecting aluminum drink cans and newspapers can be a simple, ongoing way to make money. Begin by locating your closest recycling center. Most medium-sized cities and all large cities have them. Look in your phone book under "recycle," or call the closest large city for information. Decide on a convenient time to take your cans or papers to the center. Then announce the recycling drive in the church newsletter, with drop-off dates and times. Give people three or four weeks to collect the items.

If your community is not too large, offer to pick up the cans and papers. Go to local parks on Saturday mornings or after holiday weekends to collect cans. You will be doing a service to your community and also collecting lots of money for cans. If you have a soft-drink machine in your church, you can put a large trash can marked "cans only" next to the machine. If the initial drive goes well, you may want to continue monthly. When people get into the habit of saving, you will be surprised how quickly you will have a carload.

> **Mix 'n Matchers**
>
> "Mix 'n Match" your recycling announcement with the Eco-Dinner in chapter 3!

Road Crew   Join the ranks of people who scout the roadsides for litter. Divide the group into teams and assign areas of roadway in your area to scour for aluminum cans and glass bottles. Put your "find" in big sacks, meet at the recycling center at a designated time, and redeem them. Then go to someone's house and party!

Remind everyone to be careful not to touch sharp edges of cans or bottles, and not to reach carelessly into bags to grab something. Mean little germs could be lurking there.

AND MORE . . .

- Sell **Personal Wake-Up Calls** during events.
- Sell **Back Rubs** at conferences and retreats.
- **Wash Airplanes!** Ask a pilot in your church or neighorhood how to wash a small airplane. Practice. Talk with authorities at the local small-plane airport for permission and details. Advertise well. Do good work and build a repeatable business.

CHAPTER SEVEN

MAKE GOOD PROFITS BY SELLING PRODUCTS OF GOOD VALUE

Lively sales can be fun for everyone involved. But be sure to sell only good products to provide good value for the dollar. Use the good old sales technique of telling people how they can use what you are selling, and the benefits of it. Combine enthusiasm for your goal with sensitivity for your customers (don't be pushy!), and you will keep your customers happy! *Plan and publicize well for several weeks in advance.*

Food Vouchers   Vouchers are one of the most popular and usable things you can sell. Since everyone has to eat, people who buy the vouchers are spending no more money than they would anyway! Ask pizza, burger, and other fast-food chains or grocery stores whether they provide food vouchers that can be used for fundraisers.

With the vouchers, people get $25 worth of food for $25

worth of coupons. You make a profit because the store sells the $25 coupons to you for less than $25, and you keep the difference. It works for stores because it guarantees them business. Sometimes they even add an additional enticement of a discount on certain food items. Vouchers are good to sell to the larger community, too.

Love Notes One good sales technique when you are selling fast-food coupons in an area where you see homeless people on the street is to suggest to your customers that they buy extras to keep on hand to give to people asking for food. Many people hesitate to give money, but want to do something to help. This is a perfect way!

Birthday Calendars

Here is something that congregations love to have—a calendar with the names of all the members listed on the day they were born. People are able to stay in touch and support one another, and it builds up community! Call several printing companies to find one that makes calendars. Give them a list of birthdays. They print the calendars, and you sell them for a commission. This is another great project for late November or early December, but you will need to begin well in advance of that, possibly in August or September. Begin publicity early so people know not to purchase other calendars.

Make Mulch!

If your group wants to care for the earth, this project is for you—*if* your church or organization has easy access to a place where you can make mulch! You'll need to fence in at least one, and preferably two or three areas about 5 to 6 feet long, in which to put grass cuttings, leaves, vegetable and fruit parings, manure, and anything else organic that decomposes readily. You will need several bins, so that when one gets full and is "ripening," you can begin on another. Get the whole congregation or organization involved in saving and bringing compost materials!

Mix 'n Matchers "Mix 'n Match" by kicking this money maker off at the Eco-Dinner listed in chapter 3.

After it decays, bag and sell it. This mulch is fantastic for gardens—and no artificial chemicals go into the earth!

The Greeting Card Company   Greeting cards are one of the most popular ways to celebrate special occasions. You can create cards with a unique embossed design, which requires only basic tools.

What do you need? Card designs, card paper, tracing paper, heavy cardboard, watercolor paper, masking tape, razor knife, glue, hammer, and heavy cardboard for a padded work surface.

How do you make them? Use a pencil, carbon paper, and tracing paper (dressmaker's tracing paper may do as well). Transfer the design to heavy cardboard and use the razor knife to cut out a stencil. Attach one side of the stencil sheet to the heavy cardboard base. Glue stencil cutouts on the base board. Center accurately to fit the card design over the base. Place card paper between the attached stencil sheet and base. Lightly tap around the edges of the design with a hammer. Keep tapping until the surface is raised. Remove the paper and fold the card. Make or buy envelopes, or use gummed stickers to seal the cards. For writing, use white ink and any ink-dipped pen.

Once you have completed your first sample, you will be able to make large quantities with the embossing guide. You can obtain materials in art stores or art sections of department stores. When the cards are completed, sponsor a card fair to sell them. Browse through card stores to guide you in pricing your cards. Package them attractively. Have a good time!

Children's Story Hour   Telling stories is fun. And so is hearing them. But reading a copy of your own recorded story can be even more fascinating.

An exciting project is to compile children's stories in a booklet. Talk with parents and children before beginning the project. Explain that the children will be interviewed on selected subjects. Consider seasons of the year or special holidays. Trips and hobbies can be good subjects of interest.

You also can collect poems written by children. Spend several sessions with the children to prepare them for writing. Give them an opportunity to write and rewrite. A cassette recorder may be helpful for recording stories.

After the work is completed, compile and print all the stories and poems in booklet form. Sell extra copies of the booklet to the parents. Announce the book and price during a story hour. At that time, the children may read their own stories or poems.

Distribute some copies to the schools. Place booklets in the children's wing of a local hospital. Proceeds from these booklets can be used to buy toys and books for the children's wing.

Have a Book Sale   Collecting and selling used books is an easy fundraiser. Almost everyone is looking for new reading material, and nearly every family has so many books they will never read again, they could fill a shelf. Bring all these people together with a *used book sale.* This fundraising activity helps people clear out their old books, and others may find books they always have wanted to read.

Advertise the sale at least a month in advance. Invite people to bring their books to a convenient location in the church. Also publicize the event in the community. Remember, the more people who know about the project, the more books and customers you will have.

Begin two days before the sale to sort and display the books. In many cases, they will need to be dusted before they can be displayed. Sort them into categories. Books for children and adults should be on separate tables. For adults, consider separating fiction from nonfiction, hardback from paperback. Mark prices on each volume with small Post-it Notes, or sort books by price and put up signs, such as "Each book on this table 75 cents." Books in excellent condition should be priced higher than those that are badly worn, but keep prices very reasonable.

Mix 'n Matchers Have a goodie table, too, where people can buy cookies and a drink while they browse.

Plan to have plenty of help the day of the sale. Ask someone to be responsible for setting up a cashier's table. Someone else should bring a change box and change. Keep the tables neat and attractive throughout the sale. If more books are available than can be displayed at one time, designate several members of the group to be in charge of restocking the tables as books are sold.

Straighten up and put away the tables after the sale.

Book/Record/Tape/T-Shirt Yard Sale

Several weeks before the sale is planned, run an advertisement in the church newsletter, asking people to clean out their closets and contribute used records, tapes, books, and T-shirts. Either pick up the sale items or ask people to bring them to the church. You also can collect items door to door. Advertise the yard sale with posters and signs in junk shops, record stores, antique shops, grocery stores, and college student-centers. You might also advertise in the local newspaper, the church newsletter, and the Sunday morning bulletin. Ask a local radio station to publicize the sale. Be sure to include in all advertisements the date, time, and place of the sale, and an alternate date in case of rain.

One or two days before the sale, sort and price all the items you have collected. Books should be divided into hardbacks and paperbacks, and sorted according to subject. They can be priced at about 10 percent of the original selling price. Paperbacks in poor condition might be sold by the sackful or by the pound. Records, tapes, and CDs should be sorted according to type of music—classical, rock, oldies but goodies, heavy metal, children's—and can be sold for 50 cents to $2, depending on their condition. The T-shirts can be arranged by size or according to the pictures or messages on them—states or vacation sites, rock groups, cartoon characters, messages. Price T-shirts at 50 cents to $2, depending on their condition.

On the day of the sale, arrange sale items on tables in the front yard or parking lot of the church. One or two people can be cashiers. Be sure you have money for making change.

T-Shirt Sales

Selling T-shirts will make money for your youth group and provide the congregation with a way to express pride in their church. You will need to contact a T-shirt shop that can make a stencil to be used as an iron-on transfer. The group can decide on the design for the transfer, which should include the church's name, a logo, and perhaps a brief slogan. If your church has a symbol or a name that suggests a symbol, such as "Lonesome Pine Church," you can develop an eye-catching logo. If a creative logo is difficult to find, many denominations and organizations have logos that could be used. Good color schemes are black on red, black or blue on gray, and blue or red on white.

The group will need to decide on a price. Two dollars over the basic cost per shirt is reasonable. Have an order form available with sizes as prescribed by the shop supplying the shirts. Display various sizes, with order forms accompanying them, in a prominent spot in the church building. Deliver shirts and collect money.

Visibility is the key to promotion. Wear the T-shirts at church functions. A two-month period of weekly promotion is sufficient. However, make the order forms available as long as people continue to buy. Most shops will keep transfers on file indefinitely.

Vendor Sales   Would your group enjoy participating in a summer festival? If so, suggest that they plan to set up a booth to sell popcorn.

Contact community organizations responsible for the festivals in your community and ask about procedures for setting up a booth. (Food permits often are waived for church groups, but may be required.) Check to see whether tables and tent tops are provided, whether there is a source of electricity, and whether water will be available for clean-up. Also find out about the kind of security provided and the size of the crowd expected.

See if you can find a popcorn machine like the kind used in movie theaters and by carnival vendors. If not, ask several people to bring hot-air popcorn poppers and large bowls or pans from home. You will need to buy popcorn, salt, and small paper bags. (Make sure that unused packages can be returned.)

On the day of the festival, set up the popcorn poppers and bowls. Pop and package several bags of popcorn to sell during busy spells. Work in shifts so that everyone can enjoy the rest of the festival; provide lots of ice water.

Be sure that the price is posted and is clearly visible. Appoint one or more people to be cashiers. Provide enough money to make change; the first three customers may need change for $20!

All-Purpose Garage Sale! This fundraiser can work well with one garage or six garages. Gather secondhand items and have a sale. The following time schedule will help you have a smooth running and profitable garage sale. (Note: In good weather, a church parking lot is a great sale site.) Late spring, cooler parts of summer, and fall are the best times for garage sales.

✔ *3 months ahead:* Decide dates for the sale.
✔ *2 months ahead:* Find a site for the sale.
✔ *1 month ahead:* Secure necessary city permits; recruit and schedule help from parents and youth; and ask the congregation to donate items for the sale.

✔ *1 week ahead:* Advertise in area newspapers; mark prices; organize items.

✔ *Day of sale:* Post signs on visible street corners near the sale site.

✔ *After the sale:* Schedule a date and place to sell or dispose of the leftover items.

As one possible variation, work together with a church in a low-income neighborhood. Price items very low—which helps the neighborhood, and you make a decent profit because you sell more items. Advertise that during the last 30 minutes, everything will be a nickel or a dime.

Advertise Your Church

Why not design and sell a creative bumper sticker advertising your church? Members of the group might create a design that represents several of the church's groups and activities—worship, service, fellowship. Bumper stickers can be printed for less than thirty cents each and sold for $1.00. Result: The youth group makes money, and the church is more visible in the community.

FUNDRAISING COMPANIES

One of the easiest ways to make money is to sell the products of a reputable fundraising company. Good products practically sell themselves, and very little time is required to prepare for the fundraiser. Choose products appealing enough to make people *want* to buy them—or select things that people need to buy anyway. Products always should be good quality and reasonably priced. Here are some companies that offer great fundraising programs and products that you can feel good about selling.

Environmental T-Shirts

Here is a product your friends will want to buy! These 100 percent cotton T-shirts have fantastic colorful pictures that promote the care of God's creation. They are easy to sell in local church groups, parachurch organizations, and large youth gatherings. You receive a packet with helpful ideas for making your fundraising successful. Your customers select the shirt they want from a full-color brochure of choices, and you deliver them later. For details, call Human-i-tees at 1-800-275-2638, or write them at 19 Marble Ave., Pleasantville, NY 10570.

Cokesbury Fundraising Program

A variety of easy-to-sell products and high-profit margins make this fundraiser a winner. Choose from a selection of delightful products, including a wide asssortment of candles, china, greeting cards, and magnets. They even send you a free, easy-to-follow *Fundraising Guide* to help make your efforts successful! For information, call 1-800-237-7511, go by your nearest Cokesbury store, or write Cokesbury Fundraising Dept., P.O. Box 801, Nashville, TN 37202-0801.

Children's Books

You can appeal to parents, grandparents, brothers and sisters, and doting aunts and uncles with this fundraiser! Sell colorful, high-quality children's books that are ethnically inclusive and have value that makes you proud to sell them. They are produced by the company that publishes *Highlights Children's Magazine,* and there are choices for children from infancy through middle school. You receive colorful order materials and samples of books to display. For information, call Boyds Mills Press Books at 1-717-253-1164, or write them at 815 Church St., Honesdale, PA 18431.

Entertainment Books

Similar to food vouchers, but more comprehensive, entertainment books have an extensive array of discount coupons for restaurants and entertainment options in urban areas. They usually sell very well and are super for people who eat out a lot. They even make great gifts. Since they are on a yearly cycle, you probably will want to sell them in November or December. One company you can contact is Entertainment Publications, Inc., 22125 Butterfield Rd., Troy, MI 48084 (810-637-8400).

Pecan Sales   Pecans are a very popular item before Christmas—especially if you can get fresh ones. Sell them at church and in the community. You can do it in either of two ways:

1. Many companies sell bulk quantities. You can bag your own—which gives a little more profit.
2. You can buy them already bagged. This option is a little less profitable, but much easier.

Keep in mind that the more you order, the less the cost. Experiment to see which type of pecan—chopped nuts or whole—sells best in your part of the country. Then repeat the sale every holiday season. One reliable company is Schermer's Specialty Pecans, P.O. Box 3650, Albany, GA 31708 (912-888-1143 or 800-841-3403).

Wrap It Up!   One easy way to raise money is to sell Christmas wrapping paper and accessories. People are buying wrapping paper anyway—and you are offering them gorgeous choices! The paper goes much further than store-bought varieties, so your customers also get terrific value. You can organize your sale in at least two different ways.

You could take orders ahead of time by distributing catalogues and asking customers to make selections. One combined order can then be sent to the supplier, and the wrap can be distributed when it arrives. This way, you won't end up with a lot of extra rolls.

Or take some orders ahead of time, but also order large quantities of some of the most popular patterns. Then sell the leftover rolls to last-minute shoppers. Any rolls you can't sell can be stored until the next Christmas season. For details, call Innisbrook Wraps, Inc., at 1-800-334-8461, or write them at P.O. Box 5248, Greensboro, NC 27403.

CHAPTER EIGHT

Nothing for Something

SOME FUNDRAISERS ASK FOR MONEY AND GIVE NOTHING IN RETURN EXCEPT SATISFACTION —OR HIGH SPIRITS!

S ome fundraisers are great fun to do—but don't provide anything for the people who give money, except perhaps a good feeling inside. In the fundraisers in this chapter, donations are given—either "out of the goodness of their hearts" or out of a competitive spirit! In large regional or national youth gatherings or events, these are fantastic. In the congregation or community they can be overdone, so limit them to about one a year.

Since donors do not benefit directly, be sure you maintain a high level of enthusiasm and pump up the purpose you are raising the money for—and keep pumping!

Friendship Links

TAPE TO CLOSE LOOP

This is a fun way to raise money at a large event. Cut up lots of construction paper into strips about 8 1/2 inches long and 1/2 to 3/4 inches wide. (If you have access to colored paper that has been used and is ready for recycling, use that instead.) At a large event, sell the strips for a small amount (25¢ to 50¢ each) to be made into a friendship chain. If you do this competitively, assign each group a different color and see which group builds the longest chain. If you want to emphasize community rather than competition (which I prefer), set a goal of reaching around the room, or to some other destination. Give pep talks and use incentives to entice people to give more. (See the end of this chapter for incentives.)

You will need paper, staplers, a money box, and lots of change. Advertise the times and places participants can buy strips. At those times, designated persons will sell the small strips and hang up the long strips.

Cutest Baby Picture Contest   Baby picture contests can be used in local churches, in parachurch groups, or at large events. Get baby pictures from pastors, youth counselors, popular Sunday school teachers, youth coordinators, church leaders, officers of your youth group, and anyone else who has a "simply darling" or "absolutely hilarious" baby picture they want to enter. Every picture is given a number and posted on a bulletin or poster board. (Be sure you have a list tucked away somewhere with names of the people who go with each number!)

People vote with money. Let everyone know when and where

there will be opportunities to vote. Advertise lavishly and remind people in advance to bring voting money. Announce who is ahead at least once or twice during the contest, so that people

who really want a certain picture to win can put more money into that person's pot!

When you are ready to announce the winners, do it with fanfare. You may even give funny prizes or certificates. Announce how much was raised for "the cause," thank everyone who participated, and mention what a difference will be made with their dollars.

Variations

Mount the pictures with lots of space in between, and invite people to write captions around them. Start things off with some of your own comments!

Greatest-Lookin' Legs Contest
Great at a large or small event. Select some men to be models. To show off

their legs, they wear shorts. So the audience cannot be biased, have the men appear behind a sheet that covers them from the waist up. Like the Cutest Baby Picture Contest, participants vote with money. Attach a giant number to the seat of each man's pants. Participants can remember the number to vote later, or if you have access to a camera that develops its film immediately, take pictures and put them on a poster by the voting place.

"Sweeten the pot" by requiring the winner to shave his legs on stage—or do some other crazy thing, such as eat a plate of spaghetti without hands.

Pennies into Miles

This fundraiser will work best for a group planning a mission tour or a trip to a work camp. It combines visual aids with an all-church challenge.

Have a creative cartoonist make a sturdy cardboard image of the youth group packed into a bus. Be sure to indicate the destination of the trip. For example, "Appalachia or bust!" Make the cardboard image so that it can be attached to a wall, but moved repeatedly. Double-stick masking tape is probably the best way to avoid wall damage.

Decide on the amount desired as a goal. Break it down into pennies: a $250 goal is 25,000 pennies. Then calculate the number of miles necessary to reach the destination. As an example, from Jefferson City, the capital of Missouri, to St. Louis, is about 120 miles. Divide the mileage into the total number of pennies. In this example, each mile would be represented by roughly 280 pennies.

Scale a highway for the cardboard bus to travel, perhaps around a fellowship hall or down a hallway and back. Make city-limit signs for the towns through which the group will travel. Place a large jar with an appropriate label on it in a prominent place. Ask congregation members to save pennies and deposit them in the container. As pennies are accumulated, the cardboard image travels down the pathway to its destination.

Run the project for a long time. People always have unused pennies they want to pass on. Make bank deposits regularly to keep the pennies in circulation.

Stock Sale

Raise a lot of money for a trip or an event by inviting other people to invest in your activity. This works particularly well with mission trips. Print stock certificates, to be sold at $10 a share (see illustration) or whatever figure you think is appropriate. Members of the youth group can sell stock to relatives, neighbors, other members of the congregation, co-workers

Stock Certificate

This hereby certifies that _____

is a bona fide supporter of the youth and youth mission program of

_____ *. Said support is manifested by the purchase of*

_____ *shares of stock in* _____ *and entitles the bearer of*

this certificate to a shareholders' report and dinner; unbounded appreciation,

and the knowledge that ripples will long to felt in an unknown number of lives.

Signed and sealed this _____ *day of* _____ ; _____.

STOCKHOLDERS WHO PURCHASE THREE (3) OR MORE SHARES OF STOCK
ARE FURTHER ENTITLED TO AN HOUR OF PRE-AGREED UPON SERVICE BY A YOUTH.

_____   _____   _____
Youth Group President   *Youth Group Adult Counselor*   *Youth Group Treasurer*

or parents—anyone who might have an interest in contributing toward the event.

If there have been no other fundraisers and the trip costs $150 per person, each person must sell 15 shares of stock at $10 a share. Approach the stock sale from the viewpoint of participation in the trip or event through a financial avenue. For example, twelve young people and three adults from your church may be carrying out an inner-city mission project; many more can participate in the mission project by underwriting it financially.

One approach would be to sell stock for a month. At the end of the month, the money received is totaled and divided by the number of people going. The remainder to be raised is also divided among those going. On the $150 trip, a group might raise $100 per mission team member through church sales. After the receipts are totaled and credited, each participant would be responsible for raising the remaining $50 through additional stock sales. If the trip is oversubscribed, the balance should be held for a future similar event. People funding the event will want their money spent for what they invested in.

While you are on the trip, send postcards to your stockholders. When you return, have a "Stockholders Meeting and Dinner." Invite everyone who bought stock to a potluck dinner provided by the families of the people who went on the trip. At this meeting, show slides of what was done, and ask trip members to tell about what they did and what the trip meant to them.

Penny Wars   Have two groups wage a contest over an issue, using money. Issues might include such things as whether a certain individual should shave off or grow a beard. Or groups might compete against each other on the basis of different categories: males–females, adults–youth, junior high or middle school–senior high.

Place two large bottles or containers side by side. Each penny contributed to a container counts as one positive point. However, negative points are the key to this fundraiser. Silver coins and bills count as negative points. If one group is losing, its members might want to put several dollar bills in the opponent's bottle, which would result in several hundred negative points for the other team.

Drum up enthusiasm for this fundraiser by building a lot of hype and publicity into the event. Come up with ways to fan the competition between the groups, instilling a strong desire to win. If you are doing this fundraiser in your local group, you might allow it to take place for a period of several weeks, so the competitive spirit will build over time. If you are doing it at a large event, you can raise large amounts of money during the event's duration.

"NOIDS"   What, you ask, are NOIDS? NOIDS are people who have been designated as "annoying people." At a retreat or an event, a participant can pay 25¢ to $1.00 to hire a *designated* NOID to annoy any person of their choosing. The NOID will not stop annoying a person until that person pays an amount equal to what was paid to hire the NOID in the first place! It is important to set guidelines and be sure that designated NOIDS are sensitive enough to back off if someone starts to act *really* annoyed. Make it clear that only social time is NOID-time. There is to be no NOID-ing during program times. Also establish NOID-free zones, where people can pay $1.00 to eat or visit in peace!

Sell Tickets to Non-Events   Design and make up tickets that are really gimmicky ways to ask for a donation. They are tickets to events that will not be! For instance, you can sell tickets to a Bakeless Bake Sale or a Non-Banquet. Play up funny "advantages" for the Non-Event, such as, "no need to dress up!" and "no temptation to eat lots of rich foods!" In your promotion, include prominently the reason you are raising money.

Pizza "Kickbacks"   This one is great for events attended by lots of youth who stay for at least one night. There should be enough free time in the schedule for participants to order pizza before "lights out."

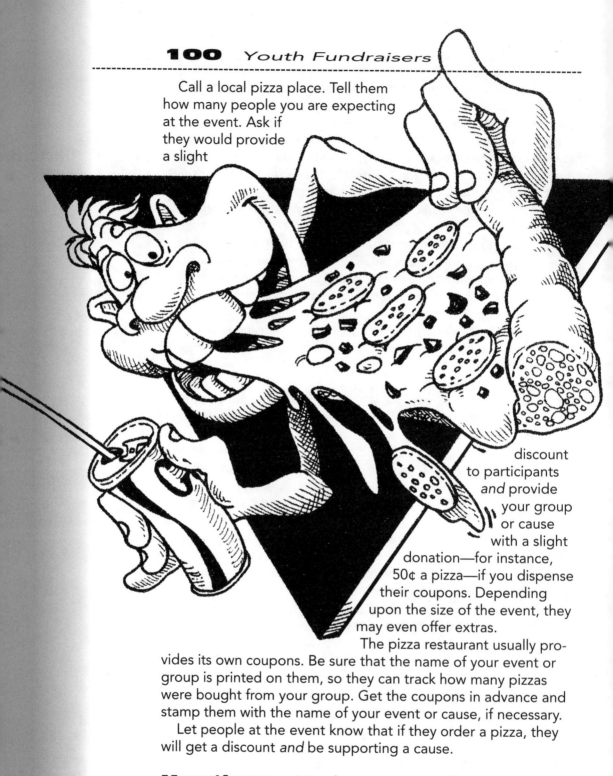

Call a local pizza place. Tell them how many people you are expecting at the event. Ask if they would provide a slight discount to participants *and* provide your group or cause with a slight donation—for instance, 50¢ a pizza—if you dispense their coupons. Depending upon the size of the event, they may even offer extras.

The pizza restaurant usually provides its own coupons. Be sure that the name of your event or group is printed on them, so they can track how many pizzas were bought from your group. Get the coupons in advance and stamp them with the name of your event or cause, if necessary.

Let people at the event know that if they order a pizza, they will get a discount *and* be supporting a cause.

Marathons   Marathons are a type of fundraiser in which you ask people for donations based upon your participation in an event. They all follow a similar pattern. Generally, marathons are events that can be measured in time or miles. They have the potential for raising large sums of money in a relatively short time. The possibilities are probably endless. Try the ones mentioned in this section, or use these suggestions to stimulate thinking for your own unique kind of 'thon! There are at least two ways to collect money for a 'thon. (*And remember to send thank-you notes!*)

1 One way to collect money: Ask a lot of people to pledge to pay you a specific amount (they decide how much) according to how you perform. For instance, if you are going to participate in a Rock-a-thon, Chris might pledge to pay you 25¢ for every hour you rock, and Lee might pledge to pay you $1.00 for every hour. After the event, you go to Chris and Lee and all the other people who pledged, tell them how many hours you rocked, and how much they owe you.

The only problem with this technique is that many people feel uncomfortable asking people for the money they pledged, or they just never get around to it. One way around this is to give the donor a slip of paper, telling what you did and what they owe. It helps to have something tangible to show! Here's another idea. Have your group figure out some ways to ask people to pay their pledge, and *practice* together! It's fun and really helpful.

2 Another way to get money: Ask for *prepaid* donations. You do not ask for so much per hour or mile or whatever. You ask for a straight donation for your participation in a designated activity. If you advertise ahead what you will be collecting for and when you will be doing it, you can remind people to bring money to donate, and you will make more money! There is a direct correlation between your success and the quality of your publicity!

Decide together how much everyone should try to get in prepaid pledges. At high-profile marathons at great big events, you can require a minimum amount of $20 to $40 in prepaid donations in order to enter. If the marathon is at the local church level, however, you may not want to require a minimum amount.

Rock-A-Thon   Young people, particularly younger youth, love all-night events, with the permission and challenge to do something that allows them to stay out late.

To prepare for this event, the following persons and items will be needed: At least five adults, one rocking chair for each group member, a television and VCR, a portable tape player, Christian tapes and videos, and snacks and drinks.

Dear :_____

The _Rock_ - a - Thon for _our mission trip to Appalachia_ is over and I rocked for _4.5_ hours!!!!! You were generous enough to pledge _$1.00_ per _hour_, which means your total donation for this event is _$4.50_. This money will help make it possible for our youth group to help others.

Your support makes a difference!

With appreciation,

Tom

(for the entire youth group)

Received _____ Date _____

Signature _____

Thank You!!!!!!!

Each group member should create a sponsor sheet. It should explain that the goal of the member is to keep his or her chair rock-ing continu-ously for nine hours— 9:00 P.M. to 6:00 A.M., Friday night to Saturday morning. The sponsors will be asked to make a prepaid dona-tion or pledge an amount per hour. Should someone make it through the entire nine hours and you are using the pledge tech-nique, the sponsor may agree to add one more unit pledge. (For example, if a sponsor pledges $1.00 per hour, and that youth rocks the entire time, he or she will net $10—$9 for each hour rocked, plus a $1.00 bonus.)

Adults should work in two-hour shifts through the night, pro-viding snacks and a planned sequence of entertainment of music and videos. They are also the monitors, to be sure no one stops rocking. Those who do stop, either by falling asleep or giving up, should stop counting their time at the last full hour rocked. They may go to sleep on sleeping bags on the floor (girls and boys in separate chaperoned rooms) or can be taken home at the next change of adult leadership. Plan to take five-minute stretch and restroom breaks every hour.

Paint-A-House-A-Thon This project is a great way to make money and help someone in need at the same time. Make a commitment to spend a day painting a house. Invite sponsors to pay for every hour your group works, or for the entire painting job.

PREPARATION

✔ Locate a house or building that needs painting. You could offer to paint the house of some needy family in the congregation or community, or some part of the church. Work out the details with the people involved.

✔ Ask a local paint store to donate the paint. They usually are willing to contribute to a worthy cause.

✔ After everyone has signed up, bring paintbrushes, rollers, drop cloths, ladders, scrapers, paint guards, plastic to protect windows, tape, and other necessary supplies. Label the items with your names.

✔ Print sponsor sheets. The sheet should tell about the youth group, the project, and the reason for raising the money. Be sure to include your name, the church's name and address, and a phone number, so that people can call if they have questions. Provide columns for the sponsors to list their name, address, phone, and the dollar amount they have prepaid or will contribute to the project.

Love Notes When you get pledges for helping needy people, think about giving the money you raise to something beyond yourselves—like a hunger or mission project. If you use the money for yourselves (like for a retreat or ski trip), then when you help a person in need, that person may feel that you do not really care. When you are helping someone in need, do it for love!

✔ Three weeks before the project date, you should begin to look for sponsors. Set sponsor goals. As an added incentive, offer a prize for the person with the most sponsors, and also one for the person with the largest amount given or pledged.

✔ After the painting is completed, send a letter to each sponsor, asking for their donation, or go in person to collect the money.

Variations

Instead of a Paint-A-Thon, have a Rake-A-Thon or a Clean-A-Thon for older people or those with disabilities in your church or community.

Move-Along-A-Thon   A Move-Along-A-Thon is a
marathon for athletes, couch potatoes, runners, walkers, wheelchairers, skaters, skateboarders, crawlers—whomever! In other
words, if you can move or be moved, this event is for you!
Usually a 2K or less event (less than 2 miles), this is a fantastic
way to raise funds for your cause. It works especially well as one
component of a very large event. It requires good advance publicity and an issue that people care about. Ask participants to
bring $20 to $40 (or more) of prepaid pledges in order to participate and get a free T-shirt.

Custom design your T-shirts and give one to every participant.
Your profit margin should still be about $15 or more per person.
Provide water at intervals along the route, and make flags for
participants to wave during the beginning "hype" and carry during the event. Begin with a pep talk by an enthusiastic emcee,
provide lively music and some cheerleaders, and invite a fire
truck and a TV crew. Ask a local fast-food place for free beverages for the returning participants.

Starve-A-Thon   This event doesn't just raise money. It
raises sensitivity about world hunger. Your youth group is locked
in the church for a 24-hour period without food. Only water or
juice can be consumed. Before you begin, talk about what it must
feel like to be hungry. Think about how being hungry will affect
you. Monitor your feelings during the experience. Expect a certain amount of irritability and be prepared to handle it! If some
cannot handle it, they can call their parents and go home. Be prepared for that. Provide games, music, and movies for fun and
distraction. Also plan time for meditation. Pray for those who live
with hunger.

Combine fun and distraction with reflection and encounter.
Some groups find it helpful to journal every two to three hours.
Verses, poems, or quotations can be prepared for those times. At
your next meeting, when your stomachs and emotions are not
growling any more, talk about the experience. What did you
learn? What is different for people who cannot go home and "fix"
the hungry feeling? This is a great unifying experience for youth
groups, and a fantastic way to raise money.

There are several good resources on hunger you might want to
use: *Children Hungering for Justice: Curriculum on Hunger and
Children's Rights,* by Carla van Berkum (specify age level), from
Church World Service (P.O. Box 968, Elkhart IN 46515-0968), and
*Hunger: Understanding the Crisis Through Games, Dramas, and
Songs,* by Patricia Sprinkle (Atlanta: John Knox Press, 1980).

Fall Rally Days

Move-Along-A-Thon

for Youth Mission Fund

What, you ask, is a MOVE-ALONG-A-THON? A MOVE-ALONG-A-THON is a marathon for athletes, couch potatoes, runners, walkers, wheelchairers, rollerbladers, skateboarders, crawlers . . . whomever! In other words, if you can move or be moved, this event is for you! A 2K event (that means less than 2 miles), it will be held on Wednesday August 7, at 12 noon during Fall Rally Days—and the proceeds go to Youth Mission Fund!!!

You'll get a custom-designed T-shirt, free drinks, the adulation of the crowds and the appreciation of the youth receiving Youth Mission grants! Lively music, an emcee, a fire truck, and maybe even a TV crew will make the MOVE-ALONG-A-THON an event to remember!

To participate, sign up at least 10 pre-paid sponsors at $2.00 each. See the registration form and flyer in this newsletter for details.

COME AND EXPERIENCE THE ONE, THE ONLY

REGISTRATION

Name _____

Jurisdiction _____

Registration Fee ($20) _____

Paid: ____YES ____NO

SPONSOR LIST

NAME	PHONE	AMOUNT PAID
_____	_____	_____
_____	_____	_____
_____	_____	_____
_____	_____	_____
_____	_____	_____
_____	_____	_____
_____	_____	_____
_____	_____	_____
_____	_____	_____
_____	_____	_____
_____	_____	_____
_____	_____	_____

"Supporting Youth Mission Fund"

YOUTH MISSION FUND MOVE-ALONG-A-THON!

_____

TIME: _____

PLACE: _____

WHO: Everyone who can move or be moved! All ages.

HOW: Get 10 prepaid $2.00 sponsors . . .
or 20 prepaid $1.00 sponsors . . .
or 5 prepaid $4.00 sponsors . . .
or however many add up to $20!

Bring your completed registration sheet and money with you to the event!

Sign-up sheet on the back of this page.
Free T-shirt to all official participants!

_____

Coordinator _____

JOIN THE FUN!!!   SPECTACULAR!!!
FANTASTIC!!!   AMAZING!!!

AND MORE . . .

- **Add a Dollar** to the cost of your event. Be sure to let people know what you are doing.
- **Have an Egg Begg.** Go to the house of a church or group member or friend and beg an egg. Take it to the house of another member or friend and sell it for whatever they want to donate. Be sure to tell them what it is for!
- Hold a **Tray Day.** Do adults in your church or organization have periodic day-long meetings, when representatives from a lot of churches or chapters come together? If they eat together in the fellowship hall, offer to take their trays back when they have finished. Before they break for the meal, announce what you will be doing and why you are raising money. Tell them that if they do not have appropriate funds, you will be happy to do it as a service, but you would welcome their donations.
- **Rent a Hug Bandit** at large youth events. For a donation to your cause, the Hug Bandit will hug any delegate or participant during breaks.
- Offer **Showers of Blessing.** For a minimum donation, a delegate/participant can designate someone—"bigwigs" included—to receive a soaking with a water-squirting toy in front of the conference. The soakee has the option of escaping the shower by paying "buy-out" money. Either way, the cause is blessed!

INCENTIVES!

Wild and crazy incentives are a super way to motivate people to give. Set your goals high, use incentives regularly, and watch momentum build! Here is a sampling to get you started.

✔ **Shave the Balloon:** The top 5 to 10 money-raising individuals or groups (depending on the setting) get to shave a water-filled balloon covered with shaving cream, held over their counselor or other consenting adult of choice.

✔ **Shave Head/Beard/Legs/Chest:** If a high monetary goal is reached, a prominent adult youth worker promises to shave in front of the entire group.

✔ **"Kidnap" a Leader:** At a large gathering, "kidnap" a prominant leader (like a bishop or minister) with their prior consent. Hold them for "ransom" until a certain monetary goal is reached.

✔ **Stocking Run:** Tie two long nylon stockings together at the toes. Every time a certain increment of money is reached, two adult leaders put the top part of the stockings on their heads and run around the grounds or church (or where ever!), tied together! You also can have a race between teams that raise the least money!

✔ **"Look, Ma! No Hands!":** The top money-raising individuals or groups get to watch their designated youth or adult leader eat a plate of spaghetti or a bowl of ice cream without using their hands.

✔ **Cross-Dressing:** If a high goal is reached, certain youth or adult leaders will cross-dress for a day.

✔ **Slime a Counselor:** If the youth reach a high monetary goal, they get to slime designated adult leaders.

✔ **Skits:** Do a take-off on a "Saturday Night Live" or David Letterman skit to motivate people to give. Make it hilarious or make it obnoxious (within bounds!). Keep repeating it until a goal is reached.

✔ **Torturous Singing:** Basically the same as the skit idea, *except* that a couple of people keep singing a terrible song until a goal is reached. It does not need to be done all at one time. In fact, it is fun to keep bringing them out at break after break, until the goal is reached.

✔ **The Silver Mile:** Someone dresses up in silver from head to foot, like the FTD florist, with wings on his head. He keeps running around and appearing in unexpected places, encouraging people to give.

✔ **Celebrity Meal:** Award "A Meal with _____" to the top one or two persons who raise the most money. The meal could be with the preacher, the bishop, a singing group at an event, or some other "celebrity."

✔ **Celebrity Photo Op:** Take a picture of the "celebrity" with the individual or group that has raised the most money, and publicize it in newsletters, on bulletin boards, and so on.

✔ **Floating Trophies:** Have a plaque, stuffed animal, or other memento (like a "Blue Duck Award"!), to be given to the person or group that raises the most money in a given length of time. At the next event, the group or person brings the award back, and *again* it is presented to the highest money-raisers. A person or group can keep it only if they continue to raise the most money. Present the award with high ceremony and hoopla!

FUNDRAISER TIMELINE

Fundrai$er: _____   Date Scheduled: _____

Responsible Youth: _____   Responsible Adult: _____

3 months prior. . .	❏	Make arrangements to use the facility or area. (Be sure no one else is planning to use it then!)

	❏	Plan details for each major work area—publicity, decorations, food, set-up, program, and so forth:
		* What needs to be done; and when?
		  (Use the "PLANNING SHEET" on page 110.)
		* What you need to get . . . and when?
		  (Use the "SUPPLY LIST" on page 111.)
		* Who is responsible for keeping the Work Teams on schedule? (Use the "PLANNING SHEET")

	❏	If a Leadership Group has been doing the work to this point, be sure the whole youth group gets involved—so more people will have a responsibility and get in on the fun!
2-3 months prior . . .	❏	Secure entertainers/speakers/special participants/suppliers.
	❏	Begin writing publicity.
3-4 weeks prior . . .	❏	Start publicizing.
	❏	Begin ticket sales.
1-2 weeks prior . . .	❏	Remind people to bring money if the fundraiser requires it!
	❏	Assemble supplies.
	❏	Reconfirm details with entertainers/speakers/special participants/suppliers.
	❏	Periodically collect money from sales.
1-24 hours prior . . .	❏	Set-up
	❏	Check microphones and AV equipment.
	❏	Put up signs.
1 day-1 week after . . .	❏	Write thank-you notes to people who helped in special ways.
	❏	Evaluate.
	❏	Collect money from pledges.

PLANNING FOR FUNDRAISER

A Planning Sheet for Work Teams

Date scheduled: _____

Work Team: _____

Person responsible for this work team: _____

Have a mental "dress rehearsal" . . . and notice details—like writing an article . . . putting up signs . . . setting up . . . making tickets . . . taking up tickets . . . pouring extra coffee . . . taking up money . . . cleaning up . . .

WHAT WE NEED TO DO Plan for *before*, *during*, and immediately *after* the fundraiser.	WHO WILL DO IT	TARGET DATE and TIME	MISSION ACCOM-PLISHED
e.g., Make sure building is unlocked	James	September 16, 9:00 A.M.	
Set up tables and chairs	John, Marlon, Kim	September 16, 10 A.M.	

Ideas for Next Time:
- How did it go?
- What worked well?
- What could be better?
- Should we do this again?

SUPPLY LIST
A Planning Sheet for Work Teams

Fundrai$er: _____ Date scheduled: _____

Work Team: _____ Person responsible for this Work Team: _____

WHAT WE NEED TO GET	WHO WILL GET IT	FROM WHERE	TARGET DATE	MISSION ACCOMPLISHED
e.g., artificial arrangement for centerpiece	Christie	Christie's mom	Sept. 15	

Have you thought of everything? Have a dress rehearsal
in your mind and notice *details*!

• *Tacks* • *Tape for signs* • *Paper bags for purchases* • *Rags to wipe spills*
• *Condiments* • *Serving utensils* • *Magic markers* • *Calculator*
• *Money for change* • *Microphone, etc.!*

Sample Thank-You Note

Sending a thank-you note to people who donate their time and money to an event is nice—and also encourages them to contribute again! If you have access to a computer, use the same basic letter for everyone, just changing the name on each one. Notes do not have to be long. Three or four sentences is great. Here are some things to include:

1. A thank-you sentence that mentions specifically what they did that was nice:

   (Thank you for . . .)

2. What the fundraiser was for and how their contribution helps:

   (Your contribution will help us . . .)

3. Another statement of apprecia-tion:

   (Your support means a lot.)

4. A personal signature:
   - by one youth on behalf of the whole group, OR
   - have everyone sign all the thank-you notes.

Love Notes Did someone do something absolutely won-derful? Pick some flowers, blow up some bal-lons, or make some slice 'n bake cookies, and hand deliver with their thank-you note!

* * * *

Here's a sample of a note that could be used for everyone who helped with a car wash.

Dear Mr. McSquirter:

Thank you for your help with our car wash last Saturday. Your contribution will help us repair the homes of economi-cally disadvantaged families in Appalachia this summer. Your support means a lot.

With appreciation,

Lindy Lewis

for "The Youth Group"

INDEX

Notes

- Recipe Book   Christmas
- peach & pecan party   June
- Bible Trivia Night   once a month
- Cake-pop sale
- Chocolate-infused
  bake off
- Taco Bar   fall
- mother/daughter tea party   Mother's Day
-